D0096952

Can America Be Saved
From Stupid People

and other essays

Dave Duffy

ISBN 13: 978-0-9718445-4-4
Copyright 1990-2007

Backwoods Home Magazine
PO Box 712
Gold Beach, Oregon 97444

For Ilene Duffy, the former Ilene Myers,
who made everything possible

Foreword

Concise, clear, and truthful. That about sums up the columns Dave Duffy has written during the past 17 years for *Backwoods Home Magazine* and the magazine's website, ***self-reliance.com.*** In an era where obfuscation and bending of the truth to suit one's prejudices is the general rule with the mass media and with politicians, I think you'll find this anthology of Duffy's columns and articles refreshing, even powerful.

The columns are primarily commentaries about current events between 1990 and the present, but his observations are so dead-on that they tend to evoke eternal truths. I doubt many people could read his "Something unsaid about Timothy McVeigh's execution" on page 183 without being disturbed deep down in the pit of their stomach, and I doubt many could read his "Sgt. Jim Duffy — an ordinary hero" on page 80 without shedding a tear for all Vietnam War vets.

Duffy continues to publish his insightful columns for *Backwoods Home Magazine*. If you're not reading them as they appear, you're missing one of life's intellectual pleasures—the unmasking of a current event for what it really is.

— John Silveira

Table of contents

Stupid people

Self-reliance

Life

Media

Terrorism and war

Guns and crime

Politics

Stupid people

Can America be saved from stupid people

(originally published in September 2000)

There are a lot of taboos, that is, things we're not supposed to talk about, in modern society. If we do talk about them we are labeled a racist or worse. One of those things is the topic of stupid people. But the topic can no longer be ignored, because for the first time in history stupid people have more political power than anyone else, and the consequence of allowing them all that power now looms like the shadow of doom over America.

To explain, a brief review of economic and political history is necessary: In the old days, and by old I mean from about the mid-17th century back, most people lived a bare subsistence existence. They spent their lives toiling to feed themselves and their families, then died young. All political and economic power was in the hands of an elite, usually a combination of clergy and aristocracy who were often the same people. Only this ruling elite was educated, and their power was typically inherited, entailing the power of life and death over poor people, who comprised 90% or more of the population. Poor people, for the most part, acquiesced in this situation, accepting that aristocrats and clergy somehow belonged in their elevated positions and that it was the poor's lot to be miserable, especially since the ruling elite assured them that heavenly reward awaited them in the afterlife. It was a great con game played by the aristocracy and clergy for hundreds of years, and it was enforced with the torture and execution of anyone who didn't go along.

But beginning in the early 17th century, advances in knowledge, in particular scientific knowledge, began a renaissance of thought, at first among a few enlightened clergy and aristocrats, that said one didn't have to live a subsistence living, that one could better one's life through the application of this new technology, that one could grow more food, heal the sick, and in general understand and harness the natural world so that everyone, not just an elite, could enjoy life.

Gradually this revolutionary idea took hold and technological advance turned into economic and political advance, and by the middle of the 18th century a significant portion of the world's civilized population, at least in western Europe, thought that every person had the right to a better life on this earth. Much of the aristocracy and most of the clergy fought bitterly against this idea, since it meant the loss of their power over poor people. But it won out anyway, with a few isolated pockets of aristocrats and clergy maintaining power over the very poorest places.

In historical hindsight, we refer to this time that ushered in a better life for everyone as the Age of Enlightenment. It spanned just about all of the 17th and 18th centuries and, in the latter half of the 18th century, led directly to America's founding with its wonderfully enlightened Constitution that guaranteed the average person the right to seek happiness on this earth, in this life. This is important, because a lot of stupid people think America sprang into existence suddenly, out of a few people's heads. It did not. It was the result of a long process of people gradually becoming aware that this life was worth enjoying and pursuing happiness in. Early Americans like Jefferson were the product of this process, and they wrote the best of it into America's Constitution.

It is also important to understand that most of the ideas that came out of the Age of Enlightenment were the product of the minds of a small portion of the population, namely some thinkers who were weary of seeing the majority of mankind living in misery. The new philosophy of that era had one goal: To make life better for the greatest number of people. Only gradually did these ideas take hold among the majority of people.

America's founders were God-fearing men, and it was generally accepted that the idea of being happy in this life, rather than waiting for the next, was in accordance with God's laws. In a nutshell, earthly misery was out, earthly happiness in, God approved of it, and so America was born.

The 19th and 20th century thus became the proving ground of how best to implement this new philosophy of pursuing earthly happiness. Two implementation systems emerged, as we all know: The welfare state of socialism, whose premise is that all wealth should be divided up among everyone evenly; and capitalism, whose premise is that individuals should be given maximum freedom to pursue their own happiness. The new country of America turned out to be the major proving ground for the latter, and history teaches us that the failed experiments of Communism and Socialism in various countries in the 20th century, coupled with the enormous success of America's capitalism, showed that America's capitalism, though not perfect, worked best.

That brings us to the present time, and you'd think we'd all be basking in the glow of the success of the Enlightenment. But enter the modern politician, a knave with a smooth voice who sees profit and political power in pitting the poor and stupid against those who have found a bit of success in the American capitalist system, and enter the appeal to the stupid that all they have to do is vote goodies for themselves and they will be delivered by the knave politician. And you have the unraveling of the America capitalist system just as the world has achieved it.

How unfortunate. The stupid have no idea how humanity got this far, how we went from a subsistence economy to America's system of bounty and relative happiness for nearly everyone. They only see the knave politician soliciting their greed and laziness. They can't understand the great struggle that produced America, but they readily grasp the concept of voting themselves unearned goodies.

And they now read this commentary and ask themselves, "What the hell is he talking about?"

Can an understanding of math and statistics save America?

(originally published in November 2000)

The other day John Silveira and I were walking by a gas station in Gold Beach, Oregon, where this magazine is located, when I remarked, "The price of gas went up again; that must be killing the motel business in this town."

Silveira replied, "They raised it a nickel. That's a dollar a tank. Most people reach their destination on a tank of gas, which means they need two tanks to get there and go back home. It's hard to believe people will change their vacation plans over an extra two dollars, yet they barely put up a fuss when the federal government takes a third of their paycheck in taxes."

"That's because people don't think like you," I said. "You consider the actual statistics involved, but ordinary people hear on TV that gas prices are high, so they change their plans. The media never mentions how high taxes are."

As soon as I said it I realized I had just discovered the Holy Grail of how to save America's freedoms from being further eroded by big government—just get them to think the way Silveira thinks; namely, with the actual numbers, the math and statistics, that apply to the decisions they must make.

Math and statistics, after all, underlie science. If a scientific theory is statistically more accurate than other theories, it is considered true enough by scientists, and they use it to advance mankind's knowledge of the world. A knowledge of statistics should work as well with social and political problems as it does with scientific problems. If all of us understood statistics, and were as honest with ourselves as scientists seem to be when they seek answers to scientific problems, I believe liberals and conservatives would see things differently.

For example, if liberals understood what the gun statistics say, namely that guns in the hands of law-abiding citizens are used two million times a year to prevent crimes, including several thousand murders and many thousands of rapes, liberals would no longer favor gun control. They would tell government at all levels to repeal the 20,000 gun laws now on the books.

Conversely, if conservatives understood what the War on Drugs statistics say, namely that the drug war has made minimal impact on drug use but has spawned numerous laws that violate our Constitutional freedoms, conservatives would no longer favor the War on Drugs. They would tell the government to free our prisons' drug offenders, who comprise 66% of our nation's prison population, giving America the highest per-capita incarceration rate in the world.

An understanding of math and statistics would also change the views of other groups in society.

For example, if senior citizens understood that the statistics on the Social Security trust fund show the fund will run out of money by the year 2012 unless federal taxes are raised on their grandchildren to about 40%, they would vote for a presidential candidate who promises to fix Social Security properly rather than one who promises to give them more benefits that must be extorted from their grandkids.

And environmentalists would look at endangered species differently if they understood that statistics show that 99.9% of all species that ever existed are now extinct, that it is nature's way of evolving. And they would act differently towards trees if they understood that statistics show that there are more trees now in America than at the turn of the century. They would tell the government to stop confiscating people's lands for national preserves that save bugs and trees.

If people understood the statistics on education, namely that the public education system is turning out high school graduates who can't read, whereas private schools turn out graduates who can, they would vote to allow school voucher programs and other types of private school funding.

In all of these areas—guns, drugs, Social Security, the environment, and education—it has been the lack of an understanding of the actual statistical evidence that has led people to make the foolish decisions they have. Doesn't that make sense?

Sure, there are other factors in there, too.

Some people, like politicians, are familiar with the statistical evidence but they choose to ignore them for selfish gain. Politicians want to get elected so they play to people's fears with anecdotal evidence about children being shot, drugs wrecking families, old people starving, old growth forests disappearing, and religious nuts educating our children. But an understanding of the actual statistics would allow people to see these anecdotal tidbits for the lies they actually are. Wouldn't it?

Am I missing something? If scientists use statistics to come up with the correct solution to problems, why don't we. Are we just stupid, or what?

Animal rights loonies save the chickens but ruin the County Fair

(originally published in November 2003)

We had our County Fair between issues.

It was a small Fair with just a few thousand in attendance, but no one in our town of 1500 would miss it for the world. There's the parade into the fairgrounds with pretty cowgirls on horses, fire engines sounding their bells and sirens, local businesses in hokey homemade floats, and all sorts of candy thrown to the children lining the one-mile route through town.

Then there's the Fair itself with its homegrown bands, immaculately groomed goats and sheep, and mouth watering blue ribbon pies. And, of course, there's midway, with its "characters" heralding the local children onto fantastic rides that come to this town only once a year. But the most popular part of our Fair is rodeo, not just because it has the real life drama of cowboy battling gravity as he rides a bronk or bull, but because at the end of rodeo comes the event that sums up the sheer delight of a small country Fair—Barnyard Scramble!

After the last bull has been ridden and the scores given out, there is a long pause before the gravel-voiced announcer suddenly bellows:

"Here it is folks, the event we've all been waiting for! Baaarnyaaaard Scraaaamble!!!"

20

Anticipating the announcement, dozens of children and their moms have already made their way down the grandstand and are crowded together at a big gate at one end of the arena.

In Barnyard Scramble, the entire rodeo arena is used to free all manner of animals, from chickens and rabbits to goats and sheep, so that first the young kids (up to age 6), then the older kids (12 & under), can chase after them and catch them. They get to keep what they catch. All the animals have been donated by local folk.

It's the real young kids that cause much of the excitement. When they are released into the arena, the cameras flash and the crowd roars with laughter as they try to catch chickens and ducks and rabbits. Mom (Dads usually stays in the stands) often has to help her youngest catch a chicken, as these birds are real tricky runners. But in the end, most of the youngsters catch something.

During the second wave, the older kids run and dive and roll around in the dirt as they try to corral everything from chickens to sheep. A fast sheep is not that easy to catch, especially when you can only use your bare hands. It is really fun to watch, and, according to my three young boys, even more fun to take part in.

Barnyard Scramble is one of those events that sets apart a small country Fair from a bigger city Fair.

But this year at the end of rodeo, the much anticipated announcement about Barnyard Scramble did not occur. The event our kids had waited all year for had been cancelled. Why? Animal rights activists in our town had simply gone to the Fair Board and convinced them that Barnyard Scramble constituted "cruelty to animals." No public debate, no sampling the opinion of the community, no testing of this "cruelty" hypothesis to see if it was true—just cancellation of Barnyard Scramble. Most Fair-goers learned of the cancellation only after they got to the Fair.

My neighbor, who is the father of two young children, summed up the general feeling in our community: "Barnyard Scramble wasn't hurtin' nuthin'. Pretty soon they'll make it so the kids can't have any fun."

It was another solid victory for the animal rights loonies, and another loss to a small community. I suppose this victory will be repeated again and again throughout America in a self-righteous effort to protect chickens and other innocent animals throughout the land.

What a shame! We are becoming a nation of sheep as animal rights tyrants and other fringe groups among us tell us how to live. I expect little protest in our community. This little writeup may be all there is. More and more, people are just accepting these arbitrary decisions forced on us by self-proclaimed do-gooders who claim to be speaking for defenseless animals. There's no science behind their claims, no give-and-take argument about what's best for both animals and the community. A disgruntled, sour-pussed organized fringe group just puts up a fuss, and a community—at least the Fair Board that's supposed to speak for the community—caves in.

I wonder if they'll cancel midway next year because some group will claim our children are somehow being exploited by the "characters" who run the rides. Got to protect the children, you know, no matter how miserable you make them. Perhaps they'll forbid all Fair food entries because that blue-ribbon apple pie might get cooked by someone who doesn't wash their hands thoroughly. Eating poison pie is no laughing matter, after all. Rodeo is a no brainer. We had a young cowboy ambulanced out of the arena this year. He was okay, this time, but maybe next time he'll end up dead. Better cancel the event now while he's still alive.

You know what I think. I think we should round up all the do-gooder loonies who insist on telling us how to live our lives and put them in a cage. Let them out only on Halloween when their once-a-year expression of their ideas will fit in nicely with all the other scary, crazy stuff, then put them back in their cage for another year so we can get on with our normal lives.

Of course, I delude myself. We can't do that. These loonies have rights. I just wish the rest of us would start sticking up for ours.

Mousers and cat loonies

(originally published in September 2003)

I must really be old fashioned. I live in the country and have plenty of rodents running around, just like many of you, so I need a few mousers to keep things under control. It's a great life for a cat. They've got so many things to hunt they hardly bother with their cat food. But the cats themselves sometimes get picked off by a bobcat, owl, or mountain lion, so you have to replace them now and then.

That's the situation I was in recently, so I looked around for a cat at an obvious place—the nearest animal shelter. After picking out a couple of nice kitties that I knew would love my barn and its inhabitants, the smiling lady cat attendant handed me a piece of paper and said I had to read and sign it. It was a contract promising not to abuse the cats. No problem; I like cats. But, above where I was to sign was a statement giving them permission for one year to come into my house any time, without warning, so they could inspect it to make sure the cats had a good environment.

I looked at the attendant with more than a little surprise on my face and read that part of the contract to her and said, "That's just a joke right?"

"No, it's not," she said firmly. "We need to know that these cats are going to a good home."

I half smiled and half laughed at her. "But you're talking about me giving you the right to come into my home, at any time, unannounced. Into my personal home?"

"That's right," she said with an authority that made me think of an old East German matron from the days when East German women athletes all looked like brick layers.

By the stern look on her face, I knew she would not be receptive to me expounding on the importance of privacy and the sanctity of one's home, so I said as politely as I could that I would try and find cats elsewhere.

A day or so later I answered an ad in the paper by a lady who was selling cats, and subsequently went to a house where at least 15 cats were crawling all over the furniture and a meekish looking husband. She wanted $10 per cat and told me the cats were accustomed to being indoors and under no circumstances were they to be allowed outside at night. Then she produced the same piece of paper that the cat lady Gestapo matron had asked me to sign.

What the hell is going on? All I want is a couple of mousers. My daughter finally dropped off a couple of cats on a visit, and they worked out just fine, until one was taken by an owl and the other by a bobcat. But they had a great life while it lasted. Of course, that's probably at least part of what's behind these cat contracts; no one wants to put the kitties at risk of being eaten by cat predators. Plus, the cat loony activists out there are probably sincerely on the lookout for people like me who insist their cats live outdoors all the time.

Here's the way I see it: Cats are predators of mice, rats, moles, gophers, and other little things that are troublesome to a country dweller like me. In exchange for their service at controlling pests, I give my cats the best cat food I can find, a nice home in my barn, and lots of pets and scratches on the head. I've had lots of cats and the outdoor ones have always, without exception, been healthier than the indoor ones.

My old cat, Champagne, was 14 when I had to have him put down because he could no longer eat or walk. But those 14 years were full of great hunting and adventure; I couldn't begin to count the number of mice he left at my front door. He wouldn't think of sleeping indoors at night, because he owned the night, prowling and stalking like the practiced feline he was born to be.

Sure, some of my other cats became a midnight snack for an owl or a roving bobcat, but that's part of the country calculation for pets. Sometimes dogs get taken by mountain lions, too. But the life these pets have while it lasts is great, surely a lot better than that of housebound city cats where they are not allowed to practice most of their instinctive hunting and stalking behavior.

These cat loonies are dooming a lot of unwanted cats with their contracts to inspect people's homes. I want cats, and so do most country folks. But the only contract we want is the traditional unspoken one whereby the cat catches pests in exchange for room and board. That's a great contract, a perfect symbiotic relationship. The cat gets to live a natural life with its occasional perils of owls and bobcats, plus they get the added benefit of contact with a caring human, which is an especially handy thing when a vet is required.

Cat loony activists need to get a life.

The Biscuit Fire — the result of environmentalism gone haywire

(originally published in November 2002)

The Oregon fire of the century occurred between issues outside the back door of *Backwoods Home Magazine*. It was called the Biscuit Fire and it consumed a half million acres, much of it prime timber, making it one of the worst fires in recorded history. My family had to leave our home several times to escape the dense smoke, and we had contingency plans to evacuate the magazine from Gold Beach, one of many communities in southern Oregon threatened by the two-month duration of the blaze.

The fire was the result of four lightning strikes, strong winds, and accumulated wood and brush fuels that quickly turned it into an intense inferno fought on a 250-mile front. Nearly 7,000 fire fighters, 40 planes and helicopters, a hundred bulldozers, and hundreds of engines fought it. For comparison, this year's highly publicized Colorado fire, the largest in the history of that state, was a quarter the size of the Biscuit Fire.

The Biscuit Fire became so big that it had to be divided into four zones—one in California and three in Oregon—with an incident commander for each zone and a unified command located in Medford, Oregon. At one point 30% of all available federal firefighting resources was concentrated on the fire. Firefighters came from as far away as Canada, Australia, and New Zealand. It cost

27

$140 million to fight and may have consumed a billion dollars worth of timber.

But that's only half the story. The fire may have been started by lightning, but the staggering dimensions it achieved was the direct result of ardent environmentalists who have unwittingly—some say purposefully—turned the nation's national forests into one big fire trap. For decades environmentalists have made it nearly impossible to do any significant logging in national forests, due to regulations that require extensive environmental impact studies before any logging can be done, and due to lawsuits filed when a timber company does get permission to log. The result is that the tree density in national forests is way beyond what it should be for a healthy forest (some pine forests have 300 trees per acre when they should have 30), and fuels on the forest floor have been allowed to accumulate to explosive proportions. The lightning strikes that started the Biscuit Fire should not have caused the inferno it did, but the accumulated "ladder fuels" quickly sent the fire into the tall timber. Strong winds and dry conditions had it spotting new fires two miles ahead of itself.

Nearly a dozen communities were threatened. In one community briefing I attended near Gold Beach, the local fire commander told the audience, "Remember, fire is a natural part of these ecosystems. Mother Nature always bats last." An angry resident shot back: "Well, we didn't have to load the bases for her."

Fire crews did a good job fighting the blaze, and grateful residents in the saved towns put up signs all over giving them thanks and calling them heroes. Unfortunately, there were no signs put up condemning the extreme environmentalists who had set the stage for this fire.

At the height of the fire, two interesting events occurred:

President Bush flew over the fire, then held a news conference at the joint command headquarters in Medford to announce a proposed forest plan that would allow limited logging with controlled underburns in national forests to prevent such fires in the future. He was immediately denounced by several environmental groups.

Almost at the same time Bush announced his forest plan, Joan Baez made a surprise visit to serenade two environmental activists sitting in trees owned by Pacific Lumber Company in California. The activists were protesting the lumber company's plans to harvest some of their own trees because they claimed it would harm the forest's ecosystem.

What a joke! Haven't any of these environmentalists looked in the mirror to see how stupid they are? Trees are a renewable resource. They grow back, for God's sake. If you allow thinning of forests, then do underburns, it's good for the forest ecosystem. Even if you clearcut, as they do near my house, you then burn and replant. It works great in Oregon. What could be more environmentally responsible? Yes, the timber companies make some money in the process. Big deal! They help the forests with their work, so they should be rewarded.

These crackpot environmentalists and tree sitters play to an ignorant audience of city slickers and college kids who can't tell a forest from a tree farm. They don't really care what is good for forests. They're just interested in pushing forward their blind agenda that Nature should not be touched under any circumstances, that it should be left for the birds and squirrels—and humans be damned. Their environmentalism is like a form of deism, and they are religious zealots who cannot be persuaded by reason, science, or common sense. They will gladly sacrifice our national forests on the altar of their ideology.

Postscript: Four years after the Biscuit Fire, lawsuits by environmental groups continue to effectively block significant salvage logging of the 500,000 acres of national forest burnt in the Biscuit Fire. Due to the delay, bug infestation and rot have made most of the timber under 20 inches in diameter worthless for commercial salvage. Of the 370 million board feet the U.S. Forest Service originally estimated could be salvaged from the fire-killed trees in roadless areas, the delays have permitted only 59 million board feet to be salvaged.

How environmental ideology hurts the solar energy industry

(originally published in May 2001)

Starting with our first issue 11 years ago, *Backwoods Home Magazine* has promoted renewable energies, especially solar energy, and for the past two years we have carried a 16-page *Energy Works* section devoted exclusively to these alternative energies.

Why? Because they represent logical choices for those of us who want to live a self-reliant, independent lifestyle, free from dependence on the electrical grid or noisy generators. For several years, *BHM* was even produced by a solar electric system.

Why, then, do I feel like I am about to travel into enemy territory because I will soon attend the solar energy industry's two largest events: Solar Forum 2001, which is the annual conference of the American Solar Energy Society (ASES) in Washington, D.C.; and the Midwest Renewable Energy Fair in Amherst, Wisconsin, which is the largest alternative energy fair in the nation.

The reason highlights a major failing of the alternative energy industry, and of the solar industry in particular: I am a political conservative, and these major solar events, and most of the corporations that take part in them, are dominated by liberal environmentalists who insist on parading their ideology in my face and in the faces of my readers.

BHM's readers not only have the use for—and the money to buy—these energy products, but they far outnumber those who buy mainly for environmental reasons. Yet, when *BHM's* readers, who are 90% conservative and Libertarian, reach out to buy a solar panel they must endure the drubbing of environmental "save the planet" messages that they view as false or hysterical.

It is to the detriment of the solar industry that this is so. These solar environmentalists, who put their ideological stamp on every news release and pamphlet that emanates from the alternative energy industry, are left over from a day when solar energy was being introduced to the world as a clean, albeit expensive, form of energy that could replace the dirty fossil fuel types of energy most of the world used. They performed a useful service for the industry then, but they are holding it back now from taking its next step into mainstream America, which is *Backwoods Home Magazine's* America.

Let's put aside arguments about the truth or falsehood of the solar industry's environmental message and consider the damage it does to solar acceptance in the rural community. Not only does the message turn many *BHM* readers off and cause them not to buy these energy products, but it perpetuates the myth that solar and other renewable energies can only compete on a "save-the-planet" basis.

In fact, solar and the other renewable energies can compete on economic and value-for-dollar bases, and that's what my readership, and the rest of America, cares about. We're not interested in environmental ideology, but in products that can help us live and raise our families. We'll take care of our own environment, thank you, without advice from people who want to take our land to save rats and owls.

In the most recent issue of *Solar Today*, the main house organ of the solar energy industry, nearly all of the articles couple solar with themes about sustainability, global warming, climate change, etc.—the usual buzz phrases about why we should buy solar products. The conference in D.C. and the MREA fair in Amherst will be full of the same nonsense. Conservatives interested in the products have to walk around holding their noses.

Let me give the solar industry a marketing tip: The American rural countryside, which is ideal for home installations of solar energy systems, is populated mainly by conservative people who want to raise their families without crime or government intrusion. We left the liberals back in the cities. That's why Bush won nearly all the rural states, and Gore won all the states with big cities where liberals and environmentalists dominate.

If you want to sell to the rural market, appeal to us. Leave your ideology behind, as it only nauseates us, and we have difficulty reaching for our wallets when nauseated.

Solar is ready for mainstream America, and we are ready for your energy products—if they are affordable and reliable. Especially if they make us more independent. Sell solar to us on that basis.

We are the people who used windmills earlier in this century. We were not buyers of ideology then, and we are not buyers of ideology now. We are buyers of products that can help us live well. It's about time you realized that.

Politically correct

(originally published in July 1991)

"Politically correct" is the new phrase in America's political jargon, especially on college campuses. In general, it means that when you speak you should refrain from using words that may be taken as an insult by a particular group. The aim is to make us more sensitive to our prejudices against various groups such as women, blacks, homosexuals, native Americans, Hispanics, the disabled, etc.

Chief targets of the politically correct movement are conservatives who are not properly sensitive to the needs of the "oppressed" and books that do not give due historical credit to minorities or women. Certain books are no longer permitted on campus, while others are being rewritten to give proper credit to minorities. Professors have even been sent to re-education courses to politically correct their thinking.

Sounds incredible to me. I like to rail against Big Government for meddling into the lives of us individuals, but here we have a segment of society that wants to send me to a re-education camp so I'll think politically correct like them. Reminds me of Germany in the 1930s. Certain books were banned then, or changed to suit the Nazi's sense of what was politically correct to them. Professors were re-educated or fired from their jobs because they didn't think politically correct.

The politically correct movement in this country would be funny if it weren't such a strong and serious movement. As it is, it's scary. If you are not politically correct in the way you speak, proponents of politically correct thinking term you a racist or capitalist, exploiter-buzz words that often send the accused scurrying for cover.

A recent letter to me from a politically correct woman began with the salutation "Gentlepersons:". I thought it was a joke, but the writer accused me of using "gender-specific language" in this magazine's articles. Gender-specific language, in case you don't know, is when you refer to someone who could be a man or woman as a "he." For example, cowboy is "gender-specific" because there were also cowgirls. The politically correct phrase is "cowperson."

All I can say is: "Wow!" Does that make me a racist?

Here's what I think: I think people who advocate politically correct ways of speaking and thinking are nuts. They are Nazis in sheep's clothing. They are trying to establish a new form of prejudice—against freedom of thought and speech—under the guise of pretending to stamp out all the old prejudices.

If their goal is to make everybody in society equal, then they are going about it the wrong way. Stifling speech and open debate about serious problems like discrimination won't solve anything. It will just keep people's emotions pent up until society explodes in a giant backlash.

Besides, I don't think people are equal anyway. Some of us are smart, some not so smart. Some of us work hard, some not so hard. Race, gender, or political beliefs have nothing to do with it.

That's just the way it is. Saying it's different when it isn't doesn't change anything.

The proponents of politically correct thinking are alarmingly ignorant of what the American Constitution is all about. To them the Constitution is a racist rag that gave power to white hetero-sexual men, but it is not that at all. It is the first successful attempt by modern man to guarantee freedom to its citizens. One of the most important freedoms it guarantees is freedom of speech.

Sure there are problems in America, and there is discrimination and prejudice against some of our citizens. But trying to root out discrimination and prejudice with a gimmick like politically cor-rect thinking is idiotic. It would make our founding fathers vomit.

Here's what one of our founding fathers, Thomas Jefferson, had to say about politically correct thinking:

"Is uniformity (of opinion) attainable? Millions of innocent men, women, and children, since the introduction of Christianity, have been burnt, tortured, fined, imprisoned; yet we have not advanced one inch towards uniformity. What has been the effect of coercion? To make one half the world fools, and the other half hypocrites."

The age of misinformation

(originally published in May 1996)

Recently, I exhibited this magazine at a three-day Natural Health Show in Pasadena, California. The show, according to its sponsors, was meant to educate people about natural alternative approaches to health and healing, which is not a bad goal. The show, however, was anything but educational. It was largely an exercise in disinformation, with many vendors handing out phony documentation backing up exaggerated health claims for their products. The products ran the gamut from cures for cancer to water that would help the drinker live for 100 years.

In many respects, the show was no different than the environmental and New Age shows I've gone to in the past. These shows, too, are largely platforms for charlatans to expound theories based on nonsense and to sell solutions based on pseudoscience. The most bizarre of the shows are the New Age affairs, where serene-looking people parade around with metal triangles over their heads, claiming to be communing with the cosmos. People at these shows are into exploring their inner and outer selves, their consciousness and unconsciousness. They like to talk in generalizations about how modern man must get beyond modern science and achieve harmony with the energy of the universe. Psychics and modern-day holymen abound at these shows.

If you'd like to see a first-hand example of what I am talking about, go into almost any bookstore and examine the plethora of books dealing with miracle cures, spirituality, and cosmic consciousness. They are not sold as science fiction, but as factual how-to descriptions of how the world really works. For those of you who understand the value of real science, that is, the science that has given us modern medicine and things like automobiles, airplanes, and computers, a close examination of this fantasy science may make you laugh. There must be a lot of stupid people out there, you might say.

It may be stupid science that these shows and books are full of, but I am meeting an alarming number of not-so-stupid people who seem to believe in some of this stupid science. Just the other day, a friend of mine who dreams of one day travelling to other star systems much like the actors on Star Trek do, started telling me that mankind must rethink science so it can get beyond the limitations of present-day science.

I asked him what he thought science was, but he beat around the bush with generalized explanations until I realized he couldn't tell me. When I tried to explain to him that science isn't some theory you reinvent, that it is a method that allows you to discover the way the real world around us works, he protested that I was thinking about science in an old-fashioned way, that the only way mankind was going to advance, both physically and spiritually, was by reorienting our thoughts towards a new reality.

This type of mumbo-jumbo made no sense to me, and I realized it was the same type of mumbo-jumbo spouted at the shows and in the New Age books. The only thing that was different was that it was being uttered by someone who I thought had both feet on the ground.

The popularity of these charlatan shows, the New Age books, and the mumbo-jumbo explanations they put forth to explain their version of reality are, I think, part of a sad epidemic that is gripping much of modern society—a reliance on information that has nothing to do with reality. It is as if the clock is turning backwards to more ignorant times when superstition ruled the world. The shows and the books, in a very real sense, are a rehash of the ancient religions and cults that once drained off much of mankind's mental resources while doing nothing to improve the lot of people.

I think it is important for all of us to keep in mind that science is not some religion that has become popular during the last 300 or so years, ever since Englishman Robert Boyle and others began using the scientific method to discover how the physical world works. Science is not something you reinvent to suit your view of the world; it is simply a method of discovering how the physical world works.

Science is based on the scientific method, which demands that theories be subjected to verifiable experiments. The scientific method can be practiced by Christians, Buddhists, Hindus, Muslims, Jews, atheists, and agnostics. A Buddhist in New Delhi performing the same experiment in organic chemistry as a Christian in New York will get the same result. It's not a matter of opinion; it's a matter of verifiable fact.

It is this scientific method that has made possible all the modern technological inventions and discoveries of mankind, from vaccines for disease to increased ways to pull food from the soil to virtually every convenience in your house that turns on with the flick of a switch. The discoverers and inventors of these wonderful things run from Louis Pasteur to Jonas Salk, and they all used the scientific method. Name me one New Age mystic who has done anything other than line his own pockets with other people's money.

This modern-day reliance by so many people on this new conglomeration of fantasy sciences is disturbing because it represents a giant leap backward for society. The scientific method is the greatest invention since fire, and we can't turn our back on it now. There are more problems to be solved, and they are not going to be solved by some New Age prophet pretending to commune with the cosmos.

Self-reliance

Self-reliance — the key to happiness

(originally published in May 1994)

The other night I had a dream I was working two jobs and earning a fabulous salary at each. The problem was I hated both jobs; in fact, I didn't even know what I was supposed to be doing at them. I went from one job to the other in a sort of no-man's land, sneaking down the hallways and wondering if I would be caught not knowing what to do. I didn't dare ask my bosses anything because I had been at these jobs for a long time, and everyone thought I was an expert.

I suspected my uselessness would soon be detected and I would be fired. Not only did I not want to lose my big income, but I dreaded the humiliation of being exposed for the fraud I was. I wanted to quit before that happened, and it became the desperate goal of my dream to find a way to quit my job with dignity and without winding up broke.

I woke in a panic, and my wife asked what was wrong. When I told her, she said she had had a strange dream too. She said that in her dream I had taken my pocketknife and slowly and carefully made a cut around my left wrist. The knife went deeper and deeper until the hand fell to the floor. She gasped and asked me why I did it, and I told her not to get excited, that it was not that important. She became very excited and she said I tried to calm her. The hand has been pretty good to me all these years, I told her, but now I would get used to not having it. "It's not a big deal," she said I told her. "Don't get worked up over nothing."

"You were so positive in the dream," she told me. "You know, like you always are."

I knew immediately what the dreams were about. For my dream, my subconscious had dredged up a ten-year period of my life that ended five years ago when I started *Backwoods Home Magazine,* and by coincidence my wife's subconscious had dredged up the five-year period of my life since I started the magazine. The ten-year period was full of self-doubt and growing dislike for the succession of good-paying but unrewarding jobs. The five-year period was full of achievement and love of my job as *BHM*'s publisher and editor.

The dreams brought home an important and eternal truth for me and, I think, for many readers of this magazine: **If you are not as happy as you think you should be, try taking total control of your life and doing what you really want to do. Try self-reliance.**

For some of you that will mean doing what I have done: Forsaking the cozy, secure, high-paying, but unsatisfying career and striking out on your own. You may fail or you may succeed, but you'll never know unless you try. If you succeed, you'll be the envy of all those who were too afraid to try; if you fail, you will simply go back to what you were doing.

I left Southern California's defense industry five years ago, at age forty-five. I left because I was growing increasingly afraid that I would not be able to keep a promise I had made to myself in my youth, namely that when I looked in the mirror at age fifty I wanted to be able to say, "Good work, Dave; you utilized your

God-given talents to the best of your ability, and you gave life the best shot you could have. Congratulations; you are a success."

Here's how I figure it: Life is a gift you should not waste. If you're lucky, you're alive for about 80 healthy years. That's the blink of an eye when compared to the couple of million years humans have been on earth, and it's an even quicker blink when you compare it to the millions of years that preceded humans and the millions that will follow them. So why waste this precious moment of life? Why throw it away on a job you hate, in a life that gives you little satisfaction? Why not go for it all?

Here's another way to look at it: Being born in itself is like winning the state lottery. Consider the hundreds of millions of sperm your father had and the several million eggs your mother's body produced. Somehow those two people met and the lucky combination that created you was one chance in billions. Talk about hitting the jackpot—just having the opportunity to be alive is an incredible gift.

So why waste this opportunity? Why not live up to your full potential to be a happy human being?

You won't be just doing it for yourself, but for your children, too. We all want our children to be happy, and hopefully, to be successful at something. That's what our own parents wanted for us. By striving to do what makes us truly happy, we not only fulfill the dreams of our parents, but we set the stage for our own children's success. They will learn from our example.

I know many readers already realize this and many have achieved happiness at their jobs and in their careers. Congratulations; you are already a success. But many of you are just as dissatisfied with your job and life as I was five years ago. You're the ones I'm talking to. You were drawn to this magazine, in part, for the same reason I started it—a yearning for the country, in part as a symbol for the freedom from all that afflicts your life.

As it was for me, the country and its requirement that you become more self-reliant may become your escape route to happiness. In the first couple of years of building my house, I also rebuilt my resolve to give life everything I had, whether I succeeded or not. You can, too.

Relying on yourself—SELF-RELIANCE—is the key.

Do I sound like a TV commercial? Well, this spiel will never make it to TV because there's no money to be made. It's free. All you have to do is decide that you want to be happy and to muster the guts to pursue it.

I'm going to turn fifty in a few weeks, and I can now look into that mirror and say I've kept my promise. Fifty is no magic number either; it just happened to be my number.

Maybe yours is forty, maybe sixty. Whatever it is, use it to win the lottery of your life.

If you want to survive an emergency, look to yourself, not Government

(originally published in November 2005)

Hurricane Katrina and its aftermath said what I could not have said convincingly in ten thousand words: The government cannot protect you in a major emergency. It doesn't matter whether it's a hurricane, a terrorist attack, or a burglar breaking into your home in the dead of night. It does not matter whether it's a Republican or Democrat in the White House. In the end, you—and only you—have the power to protect yourself and your family when everything is on the line. To assume otherwise is to dangle your family into the swirling caldron of unpredictable Nature, terrorists, and criminals.

This is not a revelation for long-time readers of this magazine. *BHM's* message for many years has been the same: To keep yourself and your family safe in an emergency, prepare now for both stay-at-home and sudden-evacuation emergencies. We even produced a book on the subject called the *Emergency Preparedness and Survival Guide*.

But you'd think from watching the TV coverage and reading all the media hysterics about Hurricane Katrina that the United States had just suffered some sort of cataclysmic failure in our political structure because the Government wasn't there quick enough to rescue all the victims of the floods.

Huh? Does the media live in Disneyland? Of course, I realize a lot of the coverage was just the left-leaning media trying to make their arch enemy, President Bush, look bad. In an effort to put lefties back in power in the White House and Congress at some point in the future, they'll gladly mislead the public into thinking Government could have and should have rescued all the victims of the hurricane and ensuing flooding.

But here's the awful truth: If a major disaster, such as another category 4 or 5 hurricane, or a major terrorist attack with, say, a dirty bomb, occurs again, unprepared people will suffer terribly just as the unprepared people of New Orleans suffered terribly. Government, at all levels, is simply not organized (it's run by bureaucracies, for God's sake) or equipped to respond quickly to large emergencies. Eventually, if you are still alive after several days or a couple of weeks, and if criminal thugs haven't found you first, some Government or volunteer rescuer will probably find you and give you some minimal help.

In the meantime, you must be able to take care of yourself for several days to several weeks if a major emergency hits. And, you may even have to take care of yourself even longer. What if the Avian Flu mutates, as some health officials fear, and becomes a major deadly pandemic? You and your family may have to hole up in your house for a couple of months to avoid becoming infected.

Whether you have to grab your 72-hour pack and leave your home, or you have to hole up where you are until the emergency passes, you can be reasonably comfortable and safe if you are prepared. It means having some obvious things like water, food, and a method of communication, and it means having some things you might overlook, such as a generator and a gun for protection against thugs.

Hurricane Katrina and the inability of Government at any level to respond in a timely, life-saving manner should set off alarm bells in our heads. If you want to protect yourself and your family, don't follow the advice of the media or opportunistic politicians by voting for a new set of politicians and asking Government to spend billions of dollars on various projects. That won't do it. Take your life into your own hands, and plan to take care of yourself and your family in an emergency situation. You, any only you, can become the timely power that will save your family when disaster strikes.

That old survivalist mumbo-jumbo makes a lot of sense to me

(originally published in January 2005)

You don't hear a lot of talk these days about preparedness. You know, storing food and water, having a generator and extra gas, keeping a grab-and-go pack with survival items in the trunk of your car, and preparing yourself for any eventuality that could come down the highway in the future so that you and your family can survive it in comfort. It all sounds like a bunch of survivalist mumbo-jumbo to most people. But, just off the top of my head, I came up with several good reasons to take another look at that old survivalist mumbo-jumbo:

1. The economy: America is in debt up to its ears. If it continues, some economists predict foreigners may lose faith in the American dollar, pull their money out, and we'll be in an instant Depression. If you're near a large population center, you could be in for trouble from desperate people pouring into the countryside.

2. Terrorism: Terrorism could visit America again, possibly in the form of a biological attack that could require us to hunker down in our homes for months. A "dirty bomb" may require us to evacuate for an extended period. A chemical attack would be less severe, unless it happened right in our town.

3. Crime: It may be down in the cities, but it's rising in the countryside because a lot of city scumbags have moved into our

neighborhoods. The farther out you live, the safer you'll be, but there are lots of self-defense measures you can take, including being properly trained in the use of a gun.

4. Inflation: It'll probably be the government's choice weapon to battle the coming insolvency of Social Security and Medicare. If inflation reaches 21%, as it did when Jimmy Carter was President, you're going to look pretty smart with a garage full of survivalist items. Even events like a severe storm can inflate the value of some items. In the wake of Hurricane Katrina, plywood jumped by $7 a sheet in one month.

5. Illness: What if a deadly epidemic like the 1918 flu came back, and there is no vaccine available to protect your family? You might have to stay home to avoid becoming contaminated with the deadly illness. Do you have enough food and supplies to do that? On a personal basis, if your breadwinner falls ill, who or what keeps the family going? If the main wood chopper falls ill, who cuts the wood for your woodstove? It's tough having a sick family member, but it's much tougher having it complicated by having too little food and other necessities in the house.

6. A personal economic meltdown: You personally could fall on temporary hard times with the loss of your income. Are you ready to weather such an event until you can get the income flowing again? If you're making good money now, pay off your debt and put some money away, either in a bank or in a drawer. (These days, your drawer pays you almost as much interest as a bank.) Save up enough to cover your mortgage payment for a few months if you have one. Stock up on food. Not only is it like having money in the bank, but it's a good hedge against rising food prices.

7. A severe winter: No one knows when the next spike in gas or heating fuel prices will occur, so it's a good idea to keep extra fuel on hand. I don't keep a big tank of gas because even with a gas stabilizer added it tends to get stale. But, I do keep my vehicles full of gas, and I have several 5-gallon cans of Stabil-treated gas, plus oil and lubricants to take care of my chain saw and other 2-stroke implements. I also have about a three-year supply of wood for my woodstoves, and a 500-gallon propane tank for the propane gas stove and the backup propane lights I had installed in several rooms in case of a power blackout. One of the best ways to deal with a fuel shortage in a cold winter is to simply stay home with your ample supplies and enjoy the wood stove.

8. It's healthy and fun: Preparedness, at least the way my family practices it, is cost effective, convenient, healthy, and fun. We seldom run out of anything no matter what my wife decides is for dinner. I date everything and rotate it with the new supplies, so it is very unusual for us to have to throw anything away. We've also got lots of frozen kale (I love kale soup...) and stored pumpkins (...and pumpkin pie) put away from this year's garden. We have a big garden and a bunch of chickens, so we eat lots of pesticide-free food and phytochemical-rich eggs.

Preparedness, I think, is one of those things you have to make part of your way of life, just like losing weight or staying in shape. I got the preparedness bug years ago, and I approach it like a game. Look around at the uncertainties in the world, and maybe that old survivalist mumbo-jumbo will make sense for you, too.

Training for the Boston Marathon

(originally published in March 2005)

Ever get a wild idea in your head that just won't go away, and you start working on it like crazy? It happens to me all the time. For the past three months I've been in training for the Boston Marathon because while jogging on my treadmill one day I got the idea that I should run a marathon, and what better marathon than the most famous of them all. Of course, I have to qualify for it first by running a lesser-known marathon under a specified time. I'll qualify at the Portland Marathon in Oregon in October so I can run the Boston Marathon in April, 2006.

Some people think I'm crazy. After all, I have no history of road racing, but have a history of back and neck problems, including a broken back and some fused disks. I've even lost an inch and a half of height as an aging adult. And I've had a mild hernia for a few years. But I'm not deterred; a good idea is a good idea.

Not all of my past ideas have been as good as this one. When I went to Las Vegas to make a living playing blackjack, I went broke quickly and ended up having to take a job as a newspaper reporter to pay the rent. Another time, I hurriedly built a second story onto my house without any plans, only to have to tear it off a year later. And in my twenties, I made detailed plans to row a boat across the Atlantic Ocean. Fellow *BHM* editor, John

Silveira, was in on that one, but another *BHM* editor, Richard Blunt, talked us out of it. It's no wonder that I've developed a reputation among family and long-time acquaintances as someone with a lot of wild, screwy ideas.

This marathon idea was off to a good start for the first three months. I steadily increased my time and speed on the treadmill from a half hour to an hour. Between it and light weights and working on a heavy bag, I got my weight down to a solid 160 pounds. But then I felt a tweak in my right ankle. It may have been just pain from the scar tissue left from a couple of broken ankles of years ago, but I apparently overcompensated with my running style and that led to my knee getting sore until finally, and suddenly, my back turned to rubber. I'm now back to walking slowly, and carefully, on the treadmill.

I haven't given up. Far from it. I've just begun to tame this idea. But a lot of other people think I'm nuts and believe it's another manifestation of my off-kilter ideas.

Wild ideas bother a lot of people, especially people who never seem to get any wild ideas. But not all wild ideas are as bad as the ones I've mentioned above. When I was 20, John Silveira and I decided to hitchhike around the country, from coast to coast and border to border. Our families were upset with us and insisted we should be out earning college tuition, but three months later we finished a 9,000-mile hitchhiking trip that we still talk about 40 years later. We rate it as one of the best things we've ever done.

And don't forget, this magazine comes from my wild idea to quit my well-paying job, move to the wilderness, and live simply and satisfactorily beyond the clutches and problems of mainstream society.

People like me who consistently conceive of wild ideas and try to carry them out are in the minority in the world. I suspect many of *BHM's* readership share my wild idea mentality because they have taken, or contemplate taking, great risks with their lives by moving into the country. Some have even thrown off their high-salaried corporate jobs and begun risky home businesses.

But the majority of people in America would consider such moves foolish. They take no chances and they act on no wild ideas that pass their way. In fact, most advocate against them, preferring instead that everyone do as they do, namely follow a safe and "sensible" path through life.

Having wild ideas is, I think, part of a philosophical view of life that says you can do anything you want with your life, no matter what the obstacles are, no matter who says you can't. You just put one foot in front of the other and your idea, or your dream, will become reality sooner or later. Giving up is not an option, but failure is acceptable so long as you go on to another equally ambitious idea.

Life is full of naysayers who say you can't move way out into the country, cut wood, grow a garden, store food, and take care of yourself and family without any help from the outside world. They've never done it, so why should you.

If you've got a good idea, whether it involves moving to the country, running a marathon, or anything else you want to do, give it a try. If you fail, learn the lesson of that failure and try again. If you realize only one of your "wild" dreams, that'll be one more than those who played it safe and never pursued their dreams at all.

Postscript: Not all wild ideas pan out, especially ones dependent on the continued smooth functioning of a 62-year-old body. By the end of 2006, my plans to run the Boston Marathon had to be cancelled after an MRI on my left knee revealed moderate degenerative joint disease. I've switched to bicycling to keep myself in shape. Maybe I'll train for the local Oregon Coast Cycling Festival race that is held here every summer. The 100-plus mile course goes right past my house.

Life

Which is better: a small town or city?

(originally published in November 2002)

Traveling has a way of giving you perspective.

For the past several summers my family and I have traveled around the country, covering as much as 9,000 miles by car in one five-week summer trip. The trips are exciting and fun, great education for my kids, and make us all realize how different our lives are from lots of other people.

Our destination is always a big city, like Boston or New York or Washington. I spent my first 29 years living in Boston, so I enjoy visiting my old South Boston neighborhood, riding the subway system I dreaded as a schoolkid, and taking in the museums and historical sites and entertainment I enjoyed so much when I lived there.

We stop in lots of small towns on the way to and from the city. Many are similar to our own Gold Beach, Oregon, a quiet, friendly town of 1,500 nestled in a fairly large expanse of open space, in our case the ocean and mountains of the Northwest.

I always gain insight into myself and my situation in life when I travel. Typically, I feel fortunate to have made the transition from city to country life long ago because I feel at home and comfortable in the country. But the city is still exciting and impressive. Here are what I see as the major benefits and draw-backs between city and small town life:

Population density: Even as you approach the city on its main freeway or expressway, cars begin crowding closer together and dart in and out of lanes in an effort to get one or two car lengths ahead of a competitor. In the country there is no such competition. Once on foot, the population of the city seems staggering to a small-town person. It reminds you of an ant colony, or a cage with too many rats.

Money: Most city dwellers would scoff at the $10 jobs that are coveted in the small town, and they would decline to drive the beat-up old pickups that seem highly prized in the country. But poverty is greater and more foreboding in the city, with its daunting tenements and sprawling slums. The best way to make money in small towns is to start your own small business, and a lot of people have done so.

Friendliness: When you walk around in the city, few people smile at you. In fact, they are likely to regard you with suspicion if you smile at them. They are not purposefully being rude, just guarded. In small towns, the friendly smile while passing is standard. And it's sincere.

Clerks in city stores are vaguely polite but not friendly. In the country, store clerks are lively and talkative. They may have children who are in the same school classroom as yours. They know your coworkers, maybe even go to your church. The women in small towns are particularly friendly and knowledgeable. They know everybody and everybody's children, often by name.

Food quality and prices: The supermarkets of a city carry a lower grade of fresh produce, it is displayed poorly, and the prices for it are higher. In small towns, the produce sections look neat, the food is fresh, and there's always fruit on sale. There had better be because often there's a farmer selling even fresher produce at his stand just around the corner.

Prices for food may be lower in small towns, but prices are higher for just about everything else. The city has the megastores with their phenomenal bargains. When the small towner needs to do a lot of heavy duty non-food shopping, he goes to the nearest city.

Tranquility: To many youngsters, the city is exciting, while the small town is boring. To adults, the city is noisy and unnerving, while the small town is calm and relaxed. In the city you are unaware of the night sky, while in the country it is obvious, huge, and black with millions of stars and several planets.

Crime: Not too far from the impressive sights of the city are the bad sections where tough-looking young men loiter. These danger zones do not exist in most small towns, and there are no gangs. The local newspapers of each locale portray things accurately: The city paper is full of murders and scandal, while the small-town paper contains grammar school and high school awards and events.

Medical care: Small towns have their GPs, but there are few specialists, even fewer great surgeons. If you get really sick, advanced medical care may be a couple of hours' drive, or a helicopter ride, away.

Entertainment: No comparison. My town doesn't even have a movie theater. We do have guest musical artists who visit town every couple of months or so. The city is an entertainment wonderland.

Community: There is a sense of order in the city, while there is a feeling of community in the small town. The best illustration I can think of are the growing number of photo-enforced traffic lights in the city. City folk don't seem to mind them, while most people in small towns would not tolerate these Big Brother robotic traffic cops.

Air quality: Boston air is not bad because it's on the coast, but most cities choke in their own filth. Small towns in valleys often have bad winter air due to woodstove fires. My Gold Beach with its Pacific breeze going down the Rogue River valley has the cleanest air in the country.

Having spent my first 29 years in the city and my next 29 in the country, which is an adjunct to the small town, I am an expert on which is best. It's the small town, in a walk.

Population density, quality of daily life, crime, air quality, friendliness, and tranquility are all important to me. I've solved the money problem by starting my own business. I'll just have to live with the inconvenience of expert medical care and lack of entertainment.

Every time I come back home from a long trip to a big city, I feel like I've just won the lottery.

"I stink!" but that's okay

(originally published in September 2003)

There are valuable life lessons to be learned from realizing you're not very good at a lot of things, even at things you think are important to be good at.

My lessons began in 1959, when I was 15. As a third-string quarterback for Cathedral High School in Boston, I really wanted to be a great football player, but as I sat in the half-time locker room of Franklin Field, with our team being massacred by powerful Matignon 50-something to nothing, things seemed bleak. Coach Tatter, who would never recognize my talents, looked down at our silent, sullen faces for only a few seconds before he bellowed, "We stink!" I can't remember the rest of the pep talk, but it was brief.

I knew he was right, and if "we stank," I must really have stunk because I was third string. Matignon, lead by future pro quarterback Jack Concannon, continued to pound us the second half, and we lost by the score of 90 to 6. The coach did not speak to us after the game, and I quit the team next year because I couldn't endure the embarrassment of being third string on a lousy team in my senior year. I wasn't convinced then that I stunk, but I had my suspicions.

Now that I am 59, and having spent a lifetime testing myself at various sports without success, I have taken up my final sport, golf, on the theory that it will reduce stress and improve my health. I had played golf years before, poorly, but this time around I took lessons from a teaching pro. It became apparent to me immediately that I was better than I had been years before. In fact, I thought I was so good that I forgot all about my stress and told my wife I would master the game, then join the Pro Senior Tour and make my retirement living that way. She believed me and bought me a set of "professionally fitted" golf clubs for Christmas.

It's been a year now, with several sets of lessons from the pro having been diligently digested and practiced, and the stress that led me to the game has been forgotten as I continue to immerse myself in the joy of playing. But my game has not reached the pro level. In fact, I am not very good at all. Progress comes slowly, almost imperceptibly, and despite my ardent practice, some days my golf absolutely stinks. At my local course, called Salmon Run, which admittedly is a tough Oregon woods and ferns-lined course where the slightest deviation from the fairway means a lost ball, I lose an average of 30 balls per round. Luckily, I've found a place to buy good used balls for 33 cents each.

A few months ago I began to suspect I would never get very good at golf. And in the last few weeks I have begun to accept what last year was the unthinkable: I stink at golf too.

But, unlike high school football where my personal esteem was founded upon youthful pursuits, I've decided it's okay that I stink at golf, and I plan to increase my participation in this enjoyable, relaxing sport.

I generally take my three young sons with me, and I pay them whenever they do well: A dollar for bogey, $2 for par, and $5 for birdie. Only one, Robby, has ever collected on a birdie, as they show signs of having talents similar to mine.

But golf got me to thinking. I've stunk at a lot of things like golf, but I've succeeded at other, more mundane things, like being a good father and a good husband.

In the sometimes difficult transition from failed high school quarterback through failed golf pro, I've finally come to understand that failure is only a rudder that steers you towards success. Each failure turned me towards something else. When I failed at football, I turned to track in college. When I failed at both track and college, I turned to U.S. Army enlistment, and when I failed at that (I at least got an honorable discharge), I became a newspaper reporter, where I finally found moderate success. Then, I became a Defense Department technical writer, with a little more success, and finally this magazine's publisher, which is a total success. I just had to be patient, I realize, not get down on myself, not blame others for my failures, and keep trying.

Mr. Tatter was right when he told us high school athletes that we stank, but he probably should have added the caveat: "But don't worry about it. Life's going to be full of these shellackings. Just go out the second half and give it all you can."

I've been examining my life with its failures and successes lately, in part because I am getting older, so I have more reason to engage in such pastimes as reflection. I think it was Shakespeare who said, "It is far better to have stunk at golf, than to have failed at life."

Or was that Homer?

Breaking a leg
and gaining perspective

(originally published in November 1996)

How often do you get the chance to relive the most traumatic experience of your childhood? I did, through the pain and terror of my 3 1/2-year-old son, Robby, who broke his right leg during a practice campout in our backyard. The campout was only 15 minutes old when he tripped over a tent rope and fell awkwardly, twisting the leg as he went down and snapping the femur, the longest bone in the body.

"I bent my leg," he screamed, and he clutched his leg, bent at the knee, and howled. I carried him in the house, and as I watched him hold tight that bent leg, I saw myself long ago as a five-year-old boy, clutching my own bent right leg in my backyard, after having been run over by an older boy's bicycle. I had broken two bones in my lower leg then, and I suspected Robby had broken at least one in his.

At the emergency room of Siskiyou General Hospital, located 35 miles away in Yreka, an x-ray of the leg revealed a long nasty spiraling break. It was evident to even a layman like me that the bone would not go back together without the two pieces first being pulled back into place. And as we wheeled Robby away from x-ray, I knew what was in store for him, and my mind drifted back to 1949 to the emergency room of Boston City Hospital as two white-clad men forcibly straightened my broken leg as I screamed.

Back in the emergency room in Yreka, a doctor and three nurses gathered around Robby, who had already been fitted with an IV that dripped morphine and valium into his arm. And the doctor turned to me and said, "You don't want to see this; why don't you take your wife for a walk."

"No, I'm staying with him," Lenie said through tears, and the doctor instructed the nurses on how to hold Robby, and then he forcibly straightened his leg as Robby screamed and, inside, I screamed all over again as a five-year-old boy.

Robby spent the next 21 days in the hospital with his leg in traction. Either Lenie or I were always with him, sleeping in a hide-a-chair a couple of feet away. The first week, the big muscles surrounding the femur spasmed again and again and sent him into a frenzy at all hours of the night, causing untold trauma among the other, mostly older patients of the ward. Other patients sent in balloons to comfort him. After the spasms stopped, he became the model patient, never complaining, almost always cheerful. He lost several of his 30 pounds of weight while confined to traction.

But, in the end, Robby is fine. He's at home for four weeks now, with only two to four more weeks before he gets his nipple line-to-toe fiberglass cast taken off, and x-rays indicate his leg is healing well.

Lenie and I are grateful, and we are humbled. During our three-week vigil at the hospital, we witnessed a lot of patients come and go. A woman younger than me died in the room next to Robby's, and a three-year-old boy with cancer cried all one night. Robby tried to send him one of his balloons, but the nurses said the boy's immune system was so weakened that they felt it unsafe to deliver it.

Three weeks in a hospital with a strictly mechanical injury puts things in perspective for parents. We knew from the beginning that Robby's injury was a straightforward fix—painful but totally doable with a high success rate.

Not so for George down the hall. After his operation, doctors told him they thought they had cut out all of his colon cancer. George was elated, until a few days later tests revealed the cancer had gotten into his lymph system, which is usually a death sentence.

Then there was Sam. He was a stroke victim who fought with the nurses during the day and called lovingly for his dead wife all night. And there was the little two-year-old girl with asthma. It took them a week before they felt they could let her go back home.

The world is full of sad stories. Most of us never see them until we are forced to. Our own writer, Lucy Shober, lost her precious child, Wren, to leukemia and is now being treated for the dreaded disease herself. My daughter Annie's friend, Nikkia, was 8 when she died in a car accident. My sister, Maureen, was 27 when her plane went down. You all have your own stories.

Bones and life are fragile, and most of us take for granted how nice it is to be alive and whole, and to have families who are laughing and growing. My family just got a reminder of how fortunate we have been.

Just Once in a Lifetime, Group of 100

(originally published in November 1991)

The way my friend, Tony Lamb of Newbury Park, California, tells the story, he was giving a guest sermon at a Protestant Church. Lamb is a Roman Catholic, and he grew up during a time when it was forbidden to set forth in a Protestant Church, but he said he didn't feel uncomfortable. "I'd talk anywhere, before any group, if I could get my message across."

His message concerned poor senior citizens, because Lamb, then 77, was the senior citizens' coordinator for Ventura County, California, a sprawling area above Los Angeles that includes 10 incorporated cities and hundreds of square miles of unincorporated areas.

He gave the congregation his usual spiel: "Poor old people are going to bed hungry at night in your community, and you should help them." Then, since it was near Christmas, he added a new twist: "This is the perfect time of year," he said. "Just once in your life reach out and help someone in need; it will be a Christmas present to yourself because it will make you feel terrific."

After the service, members of the congregation gathered around him. One man said, "I've never done anything for anyone in my life; how can I help—just once in my life?" Lamb, who never let an opportunity go by unexploited, invented a new volunteer organization on the spot. He called it "Just Once in a Lifetime, Group of 100," and it flourished for a number of years under his guidance.

The untold stories of that special group were very touching. Lamb said he limited the number to 100 to make the members feel special. Many of the volunteers who joined it not only wanted to do something for someone else, but they wanted to do it anonymously. "They just wanted to do a good deed, without the expectation of reward," Lamb said.

One old lady, Lamb recalls, lived in an old beat-up trailer. "The roof had been leaking for years," he said, "and it was hanging down on the inside. She had an old cat, named Percival the III, who used to sit all day during a rain and swat at the drops as they fell into a rusty bucket."

Lamb selected a carpenter from the "Group of 100" and asked him to rebuild the lady's roof. Money for materials came from another private fund Lamb had started to help poor seniors. "It took him a week to rebuild the roof," Lamb said, "but the satisfaction he got from helping that old lady will last him for the rest of his life."

The carpenter, as with the others who briefly belonged to the "Group of 100," was honorably and silently retired from the Group to make room for another. Lamb coordinated all the volunteers' efforts, and unlike many of the other noteworthy projects he started for poor seniors back then, he sought little publicity for the Group—"just enough to get volunteers."

Most of the "Group of 100" members did not take on large tasks such as rebuilding a roof, but did simple things. "A volunteer who does housework or who drives a car and helps an old lady get to a doctor's appointment fills an important human need," Lamb said. One women's organization helped as a unit by coordinating and transporting an elderly lady to the hospital for dialysis treatments for two months.

"Once in a Lifetime, Group of 100" was disbanded several years ago when Lamb retired for the third and final time at the age of 86, but its spirit lives on. Last Christmas, for example, Rodney Merrill, an editor for this magazine, and his wife, Kate, bought $75 worth of groceries and put them on the doorstep of a family they knew was facing a bleak Christmas. They went home and phoned the family and said, "Merry Christmas; we left a few things at your front door for you." They never revealed their identity to the family.

When Rodney told me, I could see the satisfaction and contentment on his face. He even looked younger, like he had just taken some new miracle drug that shaved several years off his age. It made me feel good just having him associated with the magazine. I'm sure Lamb would have gladly given him a diploma from the "Group of 100."

This Christmas I've decided to put the hectic pace of my life aside briefly and do something for someone else. I don't know what it will be yet, whether it will be for a senior citizen or young family, but I'm working on it. I want to get that glow on my face like Rodney had, and like the other members of "Just Once in a Lifetime, Group of 100."

You might consider joining up too. No membership fee, no forms to fill out. It's better than putting your money in the bank; it'll pay you interest of the heart for the rest of your life.

Shades of truth and sleaziness

(originally published in January 2004)

An acquaintance of mine from my years living in the city eats his dinners free from soup kitchens meant for the poor. He says the food is good and he saves at least $5 every time he goes there. Bill, a confirmed bachelor, has always been a penny pincher during the 30-odd years I've known him, so much so that he has amassed savings totaling more than one million dollars.

What's wrong here? A guy worth a million eats the free food meant for the poor so he can be worth a million five. Technically he's not being dishonest, at least by any conventional rule I can think of. No one at the soup kitchen is asking him if he is really poor, so he's not lying. And the food is advertised as free to the hungry. Bill is no doubt hungry at dinnertime. Bill thinks he's pretty clever.

But anyone looking at this situation can sense that something is wrong. Bill's behavior is at least sleazy, and probably dishonest when measured against how most of us feel people should behave.

It got me to thinking about the other borderline dishonest things in society. Take, for example, politicians trolling for votes. In the ghetto they try to spark the envy of class warfare by talking about the rich getting most of the tax breaks and the corporations gouging the poor, while in middle America they play on middle class fears of minorities by talking about fighting crime and drug abuse by getting tough on criminals and drug pushers. They're not telling lies, but they probably wouldn't interchange messages and audiences either.

The other day my local congressman, Peter DeFazio, told a group of senior citizens that President Bush's tax cuts would "quickly wipe out the Social Security and Medicare trust funds and threaten to bankrupt the country." Well, there really is no Social Security trust fund to wipe out. The so-called trust fund contains only Government IOUs that future generations will hopefully pay off. But DeFazio sees an opportunity to blame Republicans for a huge looming problem, so he uses a bit of sleight-of-hand rhetoric that seems to make sense. Not quite a lie, but not quite the whole truth.

Politicians don't have a monopoly on shading the truth. When is the last time any of us ever thought that lawyers or Government prosecutors pursued the truth in court trials? They pursue victory, not truth. The judge makes sure they don't violate any rules as they play the game. If you're rich and famous, like O.J. Simpson, you hire the lawyers who play the game best, so you win and get away with murder, but if you're a poor ignorant slob who gets caught with a marijuana joint, you automatically lose and go to jail.

How about the mass media. Does anyone still believe the mass media tries to inform us of the truth? News outlets, by and large, have their political agenda and slant the news accordingly. Just look at California's recent recall election of their unpopular governor, Gray Davis. Behind in the polls to his chief challenger, Arnold Schwarzenegger, the incumbent Governor's chief ally, the

L.A. Times, pulled out all the stops one week before the election by running a story that claimed 14 women had come forward to accuse Schwarzenegger of fondling them 25 years previous, and that Schwarzenegger was an admitted admirer of Adolf Hitler. For voters fed up with the gross distortions that had characterized the recall campaign, the *Times* story was the last straw. They threw out Davis and elected the new Governor Schwarzenegger in a landslide.

Then there's the environmental groups. Think they're after the truth? Environmentalists who fought so long to save the spotted owl admitted after they had closed down old-growth forests that the owl was mainly a convenient foil for them, that it was the trees they really wanted to save. So congratulations to them for winning. They don't seem to feel the need to apologize for using a lie to win.

No wonder Bill feels comfortable padding his million with an extra $5. It's just a game to him, just like it is for the politicians, the lawyers, the media, the environmentalists, and lots of other people. Why not grab the free meal if it's for the taking, why not shade the truth if no one holds you to a higher standard, and why not bend the rules if it means winning the game. Technically, you're not breaking any laws. But some of us still think it's sleazy and wrong.

Death

Talking to your kids about death

(originally published in January 2006)

How do you talk to a child about the death of someone they love? How do you explain the impossible? It's a task many of us parents have had to do, and between issues it was my turn.

Eighty-seven-year-old Grandma, my wife's mom, died after an illness of several months. My wife, Ilene, and her sister, Cindy, as well as three of Grandma's closest friends, were with her to the very end. They even gave her permission to die as she gasped for her last breath. "It's okay, Mom; it's okay to go."

I waited several hours to tell my three sons, Jake, 14, Robby, 12, and Sam, 10, until we came home from work and school so they could be in the comfort and privacy of their own home. They loved Grandma, and had grown accustomed to the two-day car rides we made three or four times a year to stay with her at her Oxnard, California, home. Sammy was especially close to her. During our last visit, about 10 days before she died, Sam sat on the floor and played with toys beside Grandma's bed as she waged one last fight against the ailments that besieged her frail 75-pound body. It didn't matter if there was not a lot of conversation; he just wanted to be close to Grandma.

Grandma had had osteoporosis for many years, could barely read with the aid of a magnifying glass, heard about half of what you said through her hearing aids, and breathed during the last year with the aid of an oxygen hose that was strewn about the house as she slowly trekked throughout her spacious home. A fall and a broken leg a few months ago sounded her final lap in life.

But Grandma, ever the valiant leader who had raised her four daughters alone after her husband, Jules, died of heart failure while they were still young, brought her sense of humor into her final days. A week before her death, when her daughters, sensing the imminent, converged on her home from places like Oregon and Canada, she wryly quipped, "I hope I don't disappoint you." The exhausted daughters retired to the kitchen and laughed with relief. It was their mom's way of saying she knew what was going on and she could handle it.

"But I thought she was getting better," Sam protested through his tears when I broke the news to the boys. Kids never really understand until it slaps them in the face, no matter how much you prepare them.

Their own mom had been gone for two weeks to be with Grandma. They needed a Mom hug in the worst way, but I would have to do. We stayed up late that night and had tea and cocoa in the kitchen. Between bouts of tears that sent them into the bathroom so no one could see them cry, I told them how I still talked to my Dad 41 years after he had died, and that they could talk to Grandma anytime they wanted. "She'll hear you," I said, "just like my Dad still hears me now whenever I do something I think is pretty neat and whisper, 'How'd you like that Dad?' "

I told them that at that very moment, I imagine Grandma is walking through some room where people are patting her on the back and shaking her hand and saying things like, "Congratulations, Grandma! Nice run, lady, what a life you had!

You gave it everything you had baby, beautiful, just a beautiful life." I said Grandma lived life to the fullest, raised four fine daughters, enjoyed a flock of great grandkids like them, and made the world a far better place than when she entered it. "She's done everything you could possibly do with the gift of life," I said, and I meant it. "She must be proud as heck, and we should be, too."

In the morning, the boys, resilient as children are, ate a Dad-type breakfast of fried potatoes mixed with eight eggs, onions, garlic, and fresh tomatoes they had to go out in the rain to get from the garden, and they felt fine. No more tears. Over breakfast, the boys and I, in consultation by phone with Mom, decided to plant two trees in our yard for Grandma and my brother, Jim, who also died recently.

"A weeping willow," Jake said. "And a pear tree," Robby said, "to replace the one the bear broke down." "We'll tie a hammock between them," Mom suggested.

Later in the day, during our ongoing effort to improve writing skills by having them write themes on things that interest them, I suggested they write their essays about Grandma. They took to the task enthusiastically, and it became more therapy than writing lesson. "She would make us pumkin pies. She loved to see us eat," Robby wrote. "She was working on my blankit," Sam said, referring to a blanket Grandma knitted for him as she was dying. And Jake closed his theme with, "I loved Grandma very much and no one will ever replace her."

Grandma Kathy Myers died on Yom Kippur, the holiest day of the year for Jews. Legend has it that you go straight to heaven if you die on Yom Kippur.

I can believe that! Nice run, Grandma!

Sgt. Jim Duffy — an ordinary hero

(originally published in September 2005)

My brother, Jim, died between issues. It was an expected death, as Jim suffered from lung cancer. My oldest brother, Bill, had called with the news in the middle of the night. He asked me to do Jim's eulogy at the wake.

Jim was a Marine Corps veteran who served two tours of duty in Vietnam. He was an American hero in my eyes who had endured four decades of combat-induced mental turmoil. We would honor him with a Marine Corps color guard and flag-draped coffin, and taps would be blown at his internment at the Veterans National Cemetery of Massachusetts in Bourne.

In the eulogy, with my two cousins, Dave and Chick, also Marines, serving as honor guards, I told the story of a young man who had fought bravely in battle for his country, suffered greatly in civilian life in the aftermath, yet who had retained his sense of humor through it all. Jim talked little about combat, but he liked to tell one story in particular that took place at night near Khe Sang during a ferocious battle Marines fought against a surrounding force of Viet Cong and North Vietnamese Regulars.

As Jim relates it: "I was a bit nervous. We knew the VC were all around us. I had a funny feeling, like something was near me. Then all of a sudden the bushes moved, and I just opened up and sprayed everything." He laughed every time he told the punch line: "The next morning I discovered I had killed the CO's dog; they had to hide me for three days because he wanted to kill me."

After the war, Jim never found his footing in civilian life. Like so many other vets, he drifted from job to job, found solace in alcohol and isolation, and never quite recovered. He died after years in half-way houses and finally in a nursing home. By the end, at the age of 63—a mere 23 months older than me—he was a wreck of a man, both mentally and physically.

After the phone call came from Bill, I slumped into a chair, almost relieved that Jim's ordeal was finally over. But the image that filled my mind was not that of an exhausted, defeated man, but that of Jim as a high school football hero. It was at Franklin Field in Dorchester, Massachusetts. Jim and I were playing for Cathedral High, he as the big defensive end and I as a utility quarterback waiting on the sidelines. Mission High was marching toward our end zone with the help of a short pass off both our ends. The coach called a time-out.

"We've got to stop that pass," coach said. Then he looked straight at my big brother: "Jim, try to get a jump on that pass and see if you can pick it off!" Coach had confidence in Jim's ability. We all did; he was good.

A few plays later, at our 10-yard-line, Jim leaped to his left as soon as the ball was snapped. Sure enough, Mission's quarterback had called that short pass again, but he saw Jim too late as he released the ball toward his own tight end at our goal line. Jim picked it off at the 5-yard line to avert the touchdown.

I was elated. We lost the game, but it didn't matter. My brother, Jim, was a hero. Even his response to my congratulations after the game was typical of Jim: " Yeah, so they beat us by only 33 points this time instead of their usual 40."

It was only a few years after that that Jim found himself surrounded by the Viet Cong near Khe Sang, and I think that was the beginning of the end for him. The tall, handsome end with the quick, self-effacing wit might as well have died on the battlefield, thus averting four decades of wandering, confusion, and misery.

During his final years, his brothers, Bill, Hugh, and I, made many trips to Boston to visit with him at the Don Orione Nursing Home in East Boston. Often the talk centered on our youth growing up. We were ordinary kids from Boston's Irish ghetto, Southie, and we had wonderful youthful memories of fun and daring exploits.

I look at my own three sons now, and I see my brothers and me years ago. Carefree youths. All playing one sport or another at school. Our adult lives and dreams and girlfriends all still in the future. My oldest son, Jake, is about to enter high school. He's becoming a big tall, handsome boy, just like my brother, Jim. He even has some of Jim's youthful mannerisms: The tossing of his head to the side, the quiet disposition, the well-timed self-effacing one-liner. What's to become of him? Will he, too, go off to war after high school?

Jim's service at the national cemetery was wonderful. The taps, held long by the bugler, drifted over the beautiful cemetery. On one knee a Marine presented the flag to Bill, the oldest brother: "Sir, the President of the United States, the Commandant of the Marine Corps, and the American people present this flag to you in honor of your loved one's faithful and honorable service to God and country."

The tears flowed. It was a proper goodbye to an ordinary hero.

Health

My conversation with God

(from backwoodshome.com recovery series, December 2005)

It was about 3 a.m. in the Cardiac Care Unit of Rogue Valley Medical Center in Medford, Oregon. I had already had my triple bypass heart surgery and was recovering nicely in room 3372 thanks to the skill of its medical staff and a cadre of miracle drugs like Percocet, Vicodin, and Darvocet. So I suppose this "conversation with God" might be mistaken as a brief drug-induced chat just before my head slammed into the pillow.

But it wasn't.

Crystal, the little Filipino CNA in whose arms I had briefly wept the night before in a moment of pain, twisted undersheets, and despair, had just checked in on me. She said it was very cold out and might snow. "You want I close the door?" she asked as she left.

"Yes, please," I said in a hoarse whisper. "It keeps out the noise." A hospital is never quiet with all the scuttling about of feet in the middle of the night, but there was a long pleasant silence in my room now. My room faced an expansive courtyard, and the ambient light of its tall parking lamps filled open spaces with a pleasant glow and cast fuzzy shadows elsewhere. Some brilliant young architect must have stayed up all night trying to create just such an atmosphere for its future patients. Spacious! Enough for the children and wife to keep vigil. Ilene, in fact, had slept one night on the converted sofa.

But I wasn't going to die. I had a 98-99% chance of success going into the 3-hour surgery, and Dr. Wilkinson was one of the best. "It went great," he said enthusiastically to my haggard wife, Lenie, as she first caught sight of me in the recovery room. I was decked out like some phantom rock star with jewelry made of bloody lung hoses, urine lines, and intravenous taps hanging from my jugular and wrists. The hoses flowed from under my dressing gown, gently swerving into machines that blended into the background of dozens of other recovery machines. Only my pallid face, with its breathing tube protruding from my mouth, showed starkly.

But, by now most of my tubes were gone. "This will sting a bit," Dr. Wilkinson told me while still in ICU after the nurse had surreptitiously put two vials of morphine into the IV tap in my jugular to "take away the edge." Then, he quickly ripped out a long tape that secured two bloody hoses into my midsection. I was too surprised to scream. After a moment to catch my breath, I said, "Thanks for not giving me a big description of that before doing it."

"Yeah, well," he said smiling, "there's no real way to describe what that sensation is going to feel like. Better to just get it over with. The pain will subside gradually. Besides, you look terrific. You're doing very well." And, with a wink and a smile, he was off to his next patient, an 81-year-old man flirting with pneumonia because he had trouble coughing up sputum from his lungs. He and the frantic nurses, lung therapists, and various specialists had been my companions all night through the curtained wall that separated our rooms. After we were both transferred into the

Cardiac Care Unit, I sought out the old man's room to see if he was OK. He had beaten back the pneumonia, judging by his breathing, but he seemed confused and scared, so I left him alone.

Gone, also, was my urine catheter. It stopped working in ICU, and 23-year-old CNA Lindsey, with her smiling reassuring way, slowly pulled it out after I promised she could reinsert another if I did not pee. It was the second time she had made the offer, but I had turned down the first. Now I felt more confident I could pee. It took me a while, but first a trickle, then a flood of blood-stained urine announced the beginning of my determined recovery. "Put her there," I said to Lindsey with both triumph and exhaustion in my voice, and I extended my limp, quaking hand. We shook in triumph in the first of what was to be many joyful victories during the critical five or so post-operative days of recovery.

"Pretty good pee, huh?" I said into the silence of my room. He just gave a slight nod of his head, and the half light seemed to extend into eternity. A lot of thoughts went through my mind. I felt good, almost euphoric. I had seen my three young sons earlier at a good point in my pain, so I could joke with them about all my wires leading to various video screens and all the IV lines. I described the removal of the urine catheter in terms only a boy could appreciate and laugh at. Mom then took them shopping so Robby, who turned 13 that day, could buy a present for himself. I had also talked by phone with my daughter, Annie. Due with her second child early next month, I assured her I would be back "more than 100% because a nurse told me I hadn't even known I was sick with a 90% blockage in an artery."

God just sat there, a satisfied look on his face, taking in all my excitement.

"Thanks for dropping by," I said finally. Another nod from God. He never spoke.

"Did you notice I didn't invoke your name before surgery?" I said. "Or even think about you."

Another nod.

We saw eye-to-eye on most things, even during my younger years when I denounced the Church and its priests. He saw my defiance and disbelief as a search for truth. He held nothing against me and condemned those who condemned me for not accepting their simplistic view of Him as some outlandish medieval prince who demanded blind belief, worship, and offerings.

The passing years had established our relationship. I lived by the Golden Rule, and he asked for no more. He enjoyed my sense of humor, liked the way I raised my four children. He liked my Jewish wife too, although she seemed to have a different view and relationship with him.

"That was a doozie," I said. "I felt like the Christmas turkey."

Another nod, followed by another long silence.

"I thought it might be you holding me up yesterday, when I went down the hall to see the Christmas tree. That little Cathy CNA lady came over, but I told her I was okay."

Cathy was my walking companion during two "shaking" bouts, in which my chest pain and my medication seemed to battle with each other. All the CNAs and nurses had become my anchors in this violent post-operative storm.

Now I began to nod off sleepily.

"But you sure as hell left me on my own this afternoon." I had bellowed like an out-of-control sea lion while holding my chest tight with a pillow and throwing up in a plastic basin. Nurse Steve and my friend, John Silveira, held me.

But God said nothing, merely nodding.

A long silent pause.

"But I feel good," I said. "Thanks for coming. This has been hard. I'll recover and continue as before."

Another nod from God, and this time an understanding smile. I drifted into a calm sleep, the miracle drugs having completely subdued the pain.

The day I lost my modesty

(from backwoodshome.com recovery series, December 2005)

Modesty is a hallmark for people like me who have been raised in a strict religious household, in my case a Roman Catholic home. My modesty includes a prohibition against passing gas in polite company, such as that of ladies or priests or strangers. That became a serious problem for me following my heart bypass surgery at Rogue Valley Medical Center December 1. I had gas, lots of it, for the first three-plus days after surgery. Ever backed up gas for three days? It hurts like hell, worse than the surgery even.

Since nearly everyone at the hospital taking care of me was a female, which comes under the heading of polite company, it complicated my flatulence dilemma immensely. Everything was further complicated, of course, by the fact that my muscles below were simply too weak to generate a bowel movement. Add it all up and it spells pain with a capital P.

But my modesty began slipping away after two nights of being woken by pain in my lower abdomen as the gas seemed to gurgle its way from stomach chamber to stomach chamber. I could hear it and feel it. I began asking everyone—nurses, volunteers, the doctor, family members, anyone who came within earshot—if they knew of any trick that would allow me to pass gas.

90

I even began using the word "fart," a definite no-no in polite company.

"If only I could fart, I would be okay," I'd tell anyone who would listen. It became an obsession. When one afternoon they wheeled me downstairs for an x-ray, I asked the technician there if he knew of a secret that could help me fart.

"You have any grandkids?" he asked.

"Yes, one," I said. "a little girl."

"Ask her to pull your finger," he said. I began laughing so hard I thought I would rip the stitches out of my chest. He laughed, too, and said, "Sorry, but I don't know what you can do except wait and keep trying."

The pain from my inability to fart obliterated my modesty by the end of the third day after surgery. I went from asking all females, including my wife, to leave my room so I could try and pass gas, to asking them for advice on how to fart. But it didn't matter; I was unable to generate any embarrassing air, anyway.

Finally, one day after gripping the rails of my bed, lifting my butt, and concentrating on working my fart muscles for the hundredth time, I managed a long, high-pitched fart. It brought a big smile to my face. My older brother, Hugh, who had flown out from Maryland to be with me following the surgery, saw my delight, and with a broad smile he said, "Ahhh, the inscrutable wonder of a good ripping fart."

We both laughed. That initial success was followed by five or six more over a several hour period, with each one bringing relief and a sense of accomplishment that I was finally regaining control over my life.

The next step, of course, was to have my first post-surgery bowel movement, which was a requirement, anyway, before I could go home. I made many trips to the bathroom in my room to make determined, but futile, efforts to either fart or go. I didn't care which. During one such trip, out of nowhere, I did both in one giant explosion. It was like a balloon popping; everything came out at once. I opened the door to the bathroom while still on the toilet and yelled to the several people in the room at the time: "Did you hear that?" There was laughter and applause.

And so went my modesty out the window, and it is still gone to this day. "Farting is a sign of health," my father once told me when he was very ill with cancer near the end of his life. He had just succeeded in a similar quest to fart in his hospital bed.

Fart is one of those four-letter words that entered the English language through the Anglo-Saxon tongue, I believe. (If I'm wrong, let's just pretend I'm right for a moment.) The strong, succinct Anglo-Saxon influence helps make English the colorful decisive language it is. Shakespeare sounds better in English, and in related languages like German, in part because we have this Anglo-Saxon influence with its firm, tell-it-like-it-is words. A lot of these four-letter words were so strong they became today's vulgarisms and swears. And so it is that fart has become a modern day vulgarism.

But when the going gets tough, it's nice to know there is a nice succinct and strong English word to describe just what you must do to triumph over adversity. I'm proud to be a good farter. Screw all that modesty stuff.

Stubbornness is an attribute only if tempered by common sense

(from backwoodshome.com recovery series, December 2005)

Stubbornness is typically an excellent attribute to have. It is a very close relative to self-reliance: Do everything yourself, get the job done no matter what, be persistent, never give up, etc.

I have a large dose of stubbornness in me. It's the principal reason I was able to found *Backwoods Home Magazine* in 1989 and run it these past 16 years. But stubbornness must be tempered with common sense to give it a useful direction. Otherwise, you're just a dumb mule. The other day, when I ran out of my main post-surgery pain medication in the middle of the night, I became the dumb mule.

To explain, let me first give you a brief description of the trauma that is played on the human body during open-heart surgery, which is what I underwent. Some of what I describe varies depending on various techniques you and your doctor decide upon, but this is how it often happens.

After putting you out with anesthesia, they saw your breast bone in half so they can pull your rib cage back, push aside your lungs, and work on your heart. They actually stop the heart and collapse your lungs during the operation so their movement does not interfere with the procedure. A heart-lung machine beats your heart and oxygenates your blood for you. You have a breathing hose down your throat, blood drainage hoses going into your midsection and side, a catheter coming out of your urine canal, and enough IVs to make you want to yell "Uncle!" When surgery is complete, they inflate your lungs and start your heart, bend back your rib cage and wire it together, sew you up, and begin removing all the life sustaining paraphernalia during the remainder of your 7-day hospital stay.

This operation used to keep you in the hospital for months, but now they make you get up and walk within 24 hours of surgery. In a couple of days, you are walking down the ward hallway. It can be incredibly difficult to do, but modern medical technique has shown it gets you on the road to recovery very quickly. Nevertheless, the trauma done to your body is still terrific, and doctors and nurses warn you to do the best you can with the walking, but "don't overdo it."

I seemed to progress quicker than the other patients that had open-heart surgery the same day I did. Nurses and CNAs (certified nurse assistant) were always applauding my walking. My surgeon told me the fact that I was in such good shape was "paying off big now." One nurse, however, a veteran of 37 years at this hospital, warned me that they encourage most patients to do all they can, but "with you I worry you'll do too much too quickly."

The estimated time it takes to knit your sawn breast plate is 6 weeks, and the estimated time you'll feel like your old self is 6 months or longer. You're not supposed to drive for the first 6 weeks because an accident could be catastrophic due to your sawn breast plate. My friend, Oliver Del Signore, this website's webmaster who underwent open heart surgery a few years ago, recommended I sleep most of the first two weeks of my recovery.

He said he slept the first three months in a recliner because it was too difficult to get in and out of bed.

They offer you various strong pain medications to get through this period. I chose Vicodin as my main medication, although I have several others to help with "breakthrough pain" and to "take off the edge."

When I miss my Vicodin fix, which is every 4 hours, or when the underlying pain simply surfaces too early, I hurt, sometimes to the point of tears, and the hurt is occasionally accompanied by intense and uncontrollable shaking of the leg and back muscles. (Women who have had their pain get out of control during childbirth can relate to this shaking; my wife, Ilene, had to have a spinal tap to control her pain and shaking as she tried to deliver our son, Jacob.)

So two nights ago, when I took my 2 Vicodin at 11 p.m., I was somewhat alarmed to find there was only 1 tab left in the bottle. That meant I would have only a half a dose of my main pain medication remaining for my next fix at 3 in the morning. The Fred Meyer pharmacy, located 16 miles away, didn't even open until 9 a.m. I said to myself, "Holy shit!"

So, at 6 in the morning, dismissing my wife's objections and ignoring my doctor's prohibition, I took a couple of supplementing Darvocet tabs and drove my truck to Fred Meyer. I figured I'd use mind-over-matter to control the pain by driving around Fred Meyer's tool and sporting goods departments in one of the electric shopping carts they have for disabled people. I was out the door before my wife could raise much of a fuss. She was pretty busy getting our three kids, plus a fourth kid who stayed the night, up and out the door for her 16-mile drive to school in the opposite direction.

Everything seemed to work out fine. The intense pain never materialized, I got my Vicodin prescription filled, and I even stopped for fish and eggs at the Seaside Diner, a fisherman's breakfast house. To top off a triumphant self-reliant morning, I dropped by the office of my lawyer, Pat Murphy, for a half-hour chat about guns and politics. I even bragged about being in surgery a week before, but being Irish like me he never suggested I should get the hell back home and go to bed.

When I did get home, I felt fine, but had to field a few phone calls from people like my wife and Oliver Del Signore, who admonished my "stupid" behavior. I watched Monday Night Football and went to bed (not the recliner Ollie had suggested). And I dreamed all night long that I was in some sort of machine that was rotating my body and healing it miraculously. You know how wacky dreams can be. This one just went on and on, and I was conscious of talking frequently in my sleep, while my wife, Ilene, who was trying to get some sleep beside me, asked me questions about how I felt.

Then, unfortunately, or fortunately depending upon your assessment of what was actually happening, I woke up.

It was 5 a.m. I had been in bed a restless 6 hours, and I was stiff and hurt like I hadn't hurt since just a few days after coming out of surgery.

I moaned to Lenie to help me.

She was already awake, concerned about all the noise I was making.

"Look at the chart," I said. (We were keeping meticulous records of the time and dosage of every medication I was taking.) "Is it past time for my Vicodin?"

A moment of scurrying to the bathroom to look at the chart, and then the awful response: "You have 2 hours before you're due; I gave you some during the night."

A whole bunch of colorful words came out of my mouth as I tried to describe my agony.

It took us a couple of hours to get me out of bed and ease me first onto the bathroom floor where I'd be warmer next to a utility heater, then into a chair. Lenie dressed me, built fires in our two woodstoves, and got the children ready for school. By the time they left near 8 a.m., and armed with a new dose of Vicodin, I was able to move okay, but not nearly with the effortlessness I had demonstrated while driving myself to town the day previous.

The lessons I learned? Follow the doctor's orders and listen to my wife and friends. My natural stubbornness has to give way to common sense for the next 6 months.

Contemplating the serenity of a storm

(from backwoodshome.com recovery series, December 2005)

I'm used to a very busy life. I'm a human dynamo, in fact, with more energy than just about any three people I've ever met. In the early days of *Backwoods Home Magazine*, it was not unusual for me to begin the hard mental work of preparing an issue the moment I got up, and to stop only because it was time to turn in for the night. I often went to bed anxiously because I could hardly wait to get up again and get back to work.

To say I was inexhaustible or indefatigable was to understate the amount of energy I had. Not until I met my wife, Ilene, after the second issue of the magazine was put to bed, did I finally encounter another human being who could come close to matching my ability to work. As the years went by, we became the necessary grease that assured the smooth functioning of *BHM*. Editors, writers, and staff were important, but secondary to the necessary twin locomotives who provided the sheer power to ensure the success of each issue. Magazine production, by its nature, is very difficult mental work, requiring not just skill and the ability to write and edit, but long hours of rapt attention to each of the hundreds of details that go into each issue.

I kept up my energy level for years, slowing only these last few years as the warning signs of stress began manifesting itself physically on my body. There were the skin eruptions doctors told me were strictly stress driven, and there was the racing of the heart that I suspected was my body telling me that I had better slow down, or else. So I backed out of the magazine quite a bit between issues, returning mainly on deadline to ensure each issue met the high standards I had set for the magazine.

Now I am forced to back out even more, at least during the six months following my heart bypass operation. I will write my *Note from the publisher* and *My view* columns, will edit and answer the *Letters* section, and will advise my editorial staff on key articles that could make or break an issue. Otherwise I am on the sidelines.

So here I am leading the slower, less hectic, less demanding life. I even walk slowly throughout my house, in part because my surgery scars and severed breast bone are still healing. I am redefining my role in the magazine, and in the process am discovering opportunities for myself.

It is just after 2 a.m. now, way beyond my traditional normal bedtime, but a sore body is sometimes better off sitting in a padded chair in front of a computer than trying to get an uncomfortable night's sleep lying on a pile of carefully arranged pillows on the bed. My wife is asleep just beyond the Freedom doors (some call them French doors) that separate this home office from our master bedroom. In the past, I would never have found the time to write a reflective column such as this. Time was too precious when there was a magazine to produce every other month.

But now I have time. I can write about my surgery, my recovery, my contemplation in the middle of the night of the violent storm that rages on the Oregon coast tonight. These are all important things—to me. Perhaps not so important to you. The wind that roars beyond the window a foot or so away from my right ear is typical of an Oregon coast winter storm. It has already shut off the electricity for several hours earlier this evening so that we had to go to candles, propane lanterns, and a weather radio to find out how big the storm was. It's huge, by the way, and the winds are expected to be at least gale, possibly gusting to hurricane force. The rivers, including the mighty Rogue that borders Gold Beach, the home of *BHM*, are expected to flood some areas by 3 this morning. Egad, that's less than an hour away.

It's exciting as hell, as exciting as the big Nor'easters I witnessed as a child growing up in Boston. But these storms are also very serene for me. I sit in the comfort of my well-prepared, well-stocked home and write an internet column in total security, despite the ferocious sounds I hear just beyond my window. I am sipping a glass of good Scotch whiskey, recommended by my doctor as a health drink. I do frequent "saves," just in case the power goes off again. But if it does go off, I simply resort to an old-fashioned pencil and yellow pad after lighting a couple of propane lanterns I had installed on the walls of the house a few years ago for just such an emergency.

The weather is no threat to me, short of destroying my house and rolling it down the mountainside, because I am prepared for anything, even in my present fragile condition. I have gravity-fed water from a spring, a small backup generator just in case a power outage goes on so long it threatens the frozen items in my two refrigerators, two woodstoves, and plenty of wood. (Luckily, I also have three sons who are expert at tending the woodstoves.) Plus, I have plenty of food and other supplies, reserves of gasoline, and a gun I know how to use in case I need to protect my home and family from whatever.

So I have the luxury of being able to contemplate the serenity of Nature in all its fury. Serenity is a relative word. If you are in the storm, it's not so serene, but if you are behind a window in a secure house, it's like a movie about the moods of Nature.

All the lions and bears are hunkered down asleep, along with all of humankind, except for those living in unprepared houses, which are probably scant few in this neck of the woods. I'm probably the only person awake for miles. I've even switched on my outdoor spotlights so I can watch the big firs and pines do their wild dance in the wind. Luckily, a few years ago we cut down four trees that could have fallen on the house during a big storm like this. We used to take the kids out of their bedrooms and have them sleep in a safer part of the house, but now that danger has been taken care of, so they sleep soundly through the storm in their own beds.

So, I'll wander around my house here for a while longer and enjoy the combined roar of wind, driving rain, and swaying forests. It seems especially serene to me, I think, because my body has gone through such a storm of its own. Before my surgery, I would have slept through it all.

Gaining perspective on life

(from backwoodshome.com recovery series, December 2005)

The other day, while accompanying my 14-year-old son to the Gold Beach optometry office of Dr. John Rush for an eye exam that would lead to Jake's first set of contacts, I noticed once again the citation for a Bronze Star on the doctor's office wall. The medal was for action with the 101st Airborne Division in the demilitarized zone during the Vietnam War.

I served during the Vietnam Era also, but unlike Dr. Rush's daily scrapes with death during the year he served in one of the most dangerous areas of the conflict, my job, both while stationed in Germany and in the states, involved interviewing wounded soldiers as they returned to American hospitals. I wrote Home Town News Releases (HTNR) about them that would be sent to every small newspaper in every town where the soldier had relatives. I got no medal for what I did, but I was good at it, able to write 30, sometimes 40 HTNRs a day.

The other day, Dr. Rush reiterated what he had told me on a previous visit to his office: "Your whole perspective on everything changes after going through an experience where people are trying to kill you on a daily, often hourly, basis." Since I had never been shot at, I never got that perspective during the Vietnam War. But once, while rattling off a bunch of standard questions for a standard HTNR for a wounded 18-year-old soldier in a military hospital at Fort Devens, Massachusetts, I came close. I had gotten to the question that asked, "Where were you wounded?"

There was no answer from the young soldier, so I looked up from my steno pad and he was tapping the bed sheets where his legs should have been. "Oh!" I said, surprised and embarrassed. I was actually more than surprised and embarrassed. I felt like a fool. Here I was, about as efficient as a 71Q20 Information Specialist could be, but I had become desensitized to the horrific events I was writing about. This young man—who represented maybe my twentieth HTNR of the day—had had his lower body snatched away from him. He would never be the same, no matter what assurances the Army would give him. I felt ashamed, quickly finished the interview, and wrote up one of my finest HTNRs so his relatives and folks back home could read about the heroic exploits that caused this 18-year-old to lose his legs.

But still I didn't quite get it. I was too busy! Lots of GIs were coming back wounded, so I had lots of HTNRs to write. The young soldier sank into the quagmire of too many memories and too much to do. He would surface now and then throughout my life, but not enough to really give me the type of perspective Dr. Rush had gained.

But on this visit to Dr. Rush's office, when he talked again about his perspective having changed so much from his combat experience, I realized that I, too, had finally gained the type of perspective on life that he was talking about. After being out of the Army for 36 years, my perspective had come from having my own life and death experience in the form of heart bypass surgery.

Not a very heroic way to gain insight into life and death, especially in light of the fact that I had joined the Army back in 1966 because Ernest Hemingway had said a writer needs a war experience, presumably to gain perspective on life.

I wonder if I am typical of most people: You just don't get it until you get hit over the head in a very personal way. At the age of 61, I finally understand that life and death can change places in an instant, or that you can be prematurely crippled by the failure of one of your important body parts.

I suspect I am typical of most people.

Maybe that's why many people treat war and the murders they see reported daily on TV as little more than spectator sports. A few dead soldiers in Iraq, a few gang murders in L.A.—it's all so far away and it's happening to people you don't know. It becomes just another part of the mix of entertainment we see on TV.

Until it hits home! A family member, or yourself!

Now that I have perspective on life, I doubt if I could explain it so anyone would understand. I think it's one of those things you have to experience for yourself.

When I say that I now play this delicate game of balance with my body, who would comprehend what I mean? Or if I insist that I was once hurtling full speed through life, eager to take on all challenges in my path, but am now cautious about what's under my feet when I walk, who would understand?

I'm not afraid! I'm confident in the future. It's just that I was armored in the past, and I had weapons of steel. Now I am an ordinary man with little more than a bow and arrow. Perspective such as Dr. Rush and I have gives you a glimpse into life's secrets—and ambushes. It's an education that will eventually come to you, too.

Why you may want to get a "stress test"

(originally published in March 2006)

Between issues, I underwent triple bypass open heart surgery that saved me from a major heart attack, possibly a fatal one. It was a sudden thing. One day doctors discovered several major blockages in my coronary arteries, and two days later I was in the Cardiac Care Unit of the Rogue Valley Medical Center in Medford, Oregon, after undergoing a three-hour open heart bypass surgery to correct the life-threatening blockages.

My story, and my ongoing recovery, are worth reading about because there are millions of Americans, many reading this column, who have Coronary Artery Disease (CAD) as severe as mine, but who don't know it because they have no symptoms. Heart attack, which CAD leads to unless you get your arteries fixed, is the number-one killer in America. With this brief column, I hope to alert you walking heart time bombs out there on how to detect this killer and stop him before he stops you.

Let me set the stage. I am 61, stay in pretty good shape because I exercise on a fairly regular basis, eat a well-balanced diet that pays attention to heart and cancer-healthy foods such as fish, fruits, and vegetables, take a regimen of well-informed supplements such as heart-healthy Omega 3s and folic acid, and in general pay attention to my health and weight.

But, what I hadn't considered fully when it came to my health is the importance of heredity when it comes to a healthy heart. My mother died of a heart attack at age 61, probably the same type of heart attack that was poised to kill me before my body gave me a little warning. Heredity is one of the major indicators of your susceptibility to having a heart attack, along with things like whether or not you smoke, are overweight, eat a heart-friendly diet, or have things like high cholesterol, high blood pressure, and a host of other highs that a standard blood panel will reveal. Simply getting older, like I am, is also an indicator you are at risk of a heart attack.

I typically have an annual physical, and my blood-test numbers regarding cholesterol, triglycerides, HDL, LDL, and C-Reactive Protein were always very good. Only last year did I develop borderline high blood pressure, but it was so borderline I needed no medication.

Then, one day about six weeks before the deadline for this issue, a mild pain, sort of like indigestion, occurred in my chest as I sat at the *BHM* editorial desk. It radiated out around my back, then into my jaw. I thought it was from paint fumes because someone was painting the walls in the next office over. I also had a pretty good headache.

It was four days later that I finally made my way to my doctor, John Delgado, three hours away in Ashland, Oregon. The pain had long since subsided and I felt terrific. He gave me an EKG, which showed nothing, and did a blood panel, which showed a slightly elevated cholesterol and a markedly elevated C-Reactive Protein, an indicator of possible heart attack, or its imminent occurrence.

Off to the cardiologist he sent me, who had me take a stress test, which, by the way, is the single best non-invasive test you can take to detect CAD. It indicated a probable blockage in a coronary artery going into the left side of my heart. The cardiologist had me undergo a cardiac catheterization, which is a mildly invasive x-ray test where they put a probe up an artery in the groin and thread it up and into your heart so they can actually see any blockages. The cath test, or angiogram, showed conclusively three blockages, one a long 90% blockage. Two days later I underwent my triple bypass, a major but nowadays almost routine surgery, and am now in the midst of a 6-month, anticipated to be total, recovery.

I feel fortunate to be afforded the opportunity to have a long road of recovery. Many people find out they have CAD only when they experience the surprise heart attack and drop dead. That's what happened to my mother. And I had been slipping, unbeknownst to me, ever closer to that precipice until Providence, or whatever, gave me a warning of what was about to occur.

So, here's the message: If you have any of the risk factors of CAD mentioned above, especially if you are getting older like me and have had a close relative—a parent or a sibling—who had CAD, ask your doctor if you could benefit from a stress test.

Most people don't like to think of themselves as having the potential of sudden heart attack. And the first reaction of most heart attack victims is to deny they are having a heart attack. But you may be one of the millions of CAD victims out there just days from a too-early death when it could be prevented in these miracle medical times. A stress test is easy; it will either alert you to a grave danger ahead, or it will give you peace of mind.

Love

The fishing pier

I found love on a fishing pier, when I least suspected it. I had gone there simply to catch a fish. It was a mid-November mild Saturday evening in Southern California, but most of the week-end tourists had left the Ventura Pier to escape the gathering chill. I had my Army field jacket with me, but let it lay on the wooden bench. My Irish scali kept my bald head warm. I was determined to catch a fish. My two rods were rigged the same: a four-ounce weight at the bottom with two hooks on cat gut at one and three feet, like I had always done since I was a kid fishing in Boston Harbor. But I used frozen anchovies for bait, bought at a local supermarket, not the seaworms of Boston Harbor, usually dug out of the black mud at Squantum Island.

This was the first time I had fished in 10 years. It was a brain-storm that I had to help me wind down from six months of near-ly round-the-clock writing and editing of a great new adventure with an uncertain future—a small country how-to magazine I had dredged up out of my dreams and hopes. I was giving it every ounce of brainpower and muscle I had, and I was determined it would work because I had staked my life on it, the way a prize fighter stakes his life on his only shot at a championship. I would not lose. Somehow I knew that, and I had pushed the phantoms of defeat way back into the obscure recesses of my mind.

I was fully absorbed with the fishing and checked the lines often, sometimes reeling in slowly, letting the weight drag bottom. I didn't know the fish of the Pacific very well, even though I had lived on it for the last 19 of my 45 years. But I understood fish. Back in Boston Harbor I could tell what fish I had caught long before I landed it. It was all in the hands and fingertips. Each fish had its signature that it transmitted up the line. Years on piers around Boston, and in small boats in the protected harbor, had taught me everything I needed to know. But the Pacific was different. You fish here right on the ocean, with big waves heaving your line around. Although I had caught some fish in the Pacific, and had even owned a small boat, I had always been too busy with my DOD (Department of Defense) jobs to learn about them in detail. But that would change, starting tonight.

I hummed as I watched the long gentle swells. The previous six months had been as exhilarating as they had been difficult, filled with 18 and 20-hour days at the computer trying to figure out what the content of the magazine should be, how the articles should be written and edited. I had named the enterprise *Backwoods Home Magazine*, after the 1,000-square-foot home I had built in the Siskiyou Mountains of the Oregon wilderness during the previous five years, using money earned from DOD contractors and time taken between jobs. I would quit one DOD job, drive the 670 miles to my Oregon homestead, build like crazy for two or three weeks, then return home and get a job with another defense contractor. There were plenty of jobs because Reagan was building up our military capability, and I had good skills as a technical manual editor. I figured to have my homestead finished and the magazine rolling along well before my job-hopping caught up with me. I hated the DOD industry, with its built-in waste and inefficiency, and its pompous and incompetent government bureaucrats who would not be tolerated in private industry. But the money was easy and convenient for my purposes.

I caught a small cabezon, which I wouldn't learn until years later was a good-eating fish. It looked like a brightly colored sculpin to me, and its sharp fins that stuck out in all directions would stick you easily unless you paid close attention. I took out the hook with my pliers and threw it back. I didn't want to cook a fish anyway. My 7-year-old daughter, Annie, was at her Mom's house so I'd probably open a can of something.

When I had Annie with me, which was better than half the time, we'd sometimes get a nice steak and I'd fry it up. She'd set the table with pretty napkins. We had lived in a 26-foot trailer for most of her young life, but I had recently moved into a converted garage in Ventura and parked the trailer in the driveway. It was a big step up for us, as the trailer and old GMC truck that pulled it were getting worn out from five years of hauling it to and from the Oregon homestead. The converted garage was a bicycle ride to the Ventura Pier, which we made often.

The trips to Oregon in the trailer had always been great fun for us—camping anywhere that suited us, me cooking a can of something up on the trailer stove, Annie playing with her dolls. Sometimes I read her a bedtime story, but often I'd just make up a story about the wilderness and the animals who lived in it and what our Oregon house would be like when it was all done. She'd always ask me questions about the story, so I'd have to add to it, elaborating and expanding on the dreams that were clear in my own head. She loved them. But now the house was habitable, so we could leave the trailer behind when we went there.

Annie was helping me build the Oregon house and publish the magazine. I put protective glasses on her when she was five and taught her how to hammer 16d nails into the ¾-inch tongue and groove plywood that would be our wilderness home's subfloor. It would take her 5 minutes using her two-handed grasp to drive a nail home, but she was persistent. I remember our first night sleeping in the nearly completed house. It was late spring, only half the roof was on, and it snowed. We huddled up on one side of the room, by the old Ben Franklin stove I had retrieved from a dilapidated outbuilding on the site, while the other half of the house filled up with snow. In the morning I shoveled out the house while Annie played by the fire. The day turned sunny, dried out the house, and we thought it was great fun. Annie and I were more than father and daughter; we were best friends. We loved being together.

Another bite, another small cabezon. It was a calm, thoughtful night. No wind meant the fish would probably bite. I took a bottle of Corona from my small cooler. Between it and the fishing, I was beginning to relax.

My mind and body had been wound too tight by the nonstop work on the magazine. I knew I needed some sort of break. People had always told me that I had "too much" energy, and I had tapped into my reservoir to the max to create the first two issues of the magazine.

The first issue, dated October/November 1989, was 40 pages long and filled with articles written mainly by me under five pseudonyms. My friends, Jan Cook, Leo Aaltonen, and John Silveira also contributed, and Kurt Warner, a local businessman friend of mine, let me use his office and laserjet printer to make masters for the printer.

My artist friend from DOD, Don Childers, illustrated the articles, poems, and short story. Don, like me, was another guy with dreams never quite realized. He worked for free, hoping somehow there'd be a future payoff. I gave him a 6% share of the magazine. Don was an accomplished artist, but in the preceding 20 or so years he had to content himself with doing isometric diagrams of military equipment for DOD. I wanted to utilize his real talent as an artist to illustrate articles, and he would work into the night with me trying to get the illustrations right.

We anchored that first issue with my article about the Oregon house Annie and I were building. It was titled "A Little Knowledge and Sweat Can Build a Home for under $10,000," and Don's beautiful black and white drawing set it off perfectly and it became the issue's cover. It was the first of 17 years' worth of his drawings as the magazine's covers.

Annie and I took that first issue and stuffed them into rural mail boxes along the road to Ojai, and we dropped many more on the doorsteps of houses in Ventura and Oxnard. I had paid to have 6,000 copies printed at the Ojai Valley News, a small weekly newspaper, and we gave nearly all of them away. I'm sure most were just tossed into the trash when people found them. We did the same with the second issue, which featured a wider variety of authors, including several by Rodney Merrill who would become a mainstay of the magazine for several issues.

But the work was hard. I had to learn Ventura Publisher, the complicated desktop publishing program I used to lay out the magazine, as I went. The hours were intense. I worked until I could no longer work, went to sleep, then woke and began working again on a cup of coffee. Only Annie's needs interrupted me. I had to get her to school, feed her, and read her nighttime stories. She entertained herself as I worked, drawing pictures on the backs of discarded drafts of articles. Now I needed to wind down from the tight spring I had set inside me. Fishing on Ventura's long pier, the longest in California between the times it gets blown apart by storms, sounded better than a doctor's tranquilizer.

It was getting a bit brisker on the pier now. The sun had nearly settled on the horizon. I rested my arms on the wooden railing and watched. Big long rolling swells made their way onto the beach. I thought about the last five years since my divorce from Annie's mom. The bitterness was finally gone, and I was ready for something new. Life seemed fresh.

The sun was now sitting on the horizon. It was beautiful. I took a deep breath and felt like I could conquer the world. I wanted to give out a Tarzan yell, like I often did from my Oregon porch. That's when I saw her walking down the pier towards me. A brown-haired pretty woman in jeans and T-shirt with tons of curls. She had an open black corduroy jacket for the cold. She stopped at the railing no more than 10 feet from me, a step or two away from one of my fishing poles.

It had been five years since I had anything to do with a woman, beyond a casual date or two, and I wasn't looking for romance now. But I watched the sun set with one eye and with the other I watched her. She was about 30, I guessed. Nicely built. The sky filled with a crimson glow as the sun dipped into the Pacific. One could have mistaken the spectacle as a sign from the gods. It was magnificent, one of those sunsets where conditions have to be just right. Then I walked over to my fishing pole and felt the

116

taughtness of the line. I began reeling it in slowly, then turned to her and said, "Beautiful, isn't it?"

"Very," she said and smiled at me like she was right at home.

"You came out to watch it set?" I asked her.

"Yeah," she said. "I was about to kick myself because I thought I had missed it."

I don't remember many of the details of what happened after that. We just talked. She was a kindergarten school teacher who occasionally walked out on the Ventura Pier to watch the sun set, and I was the confident new publisher who was going to set the world on fire. It was an electric atmosphere—the sky glowing, her beautiful smile, the rolling swells beneath us. I asked her to hold one of my fishing rods and right away she caught a cabezon. She was thrilled. I was ecstatic.

"That's the second fish I ever caught," she exclaimed delightedly. "My first was with my Dad when I was a kid."

I beamed from ear to ear. We talked and fished until dark, then I suggested we go back to my nearby apartment to get something to eat, then come back to the pier and fish the night away. She followed me home, we ate sandwiches, then returned to the pier in my truck. We talked and fished a couple of more hours, then I took her back to my apartment. We talked until midnight, mainly me telling her about the Oregon house, the magazine, Annie, and my plans to move to the woods. By midnight she said she had to go home.

"Thanks for letting me catch a fish," she said as she walked toward the door.

"You're welcome," I replied. Then, with a burst of courage and confidence, I said "Would you mind if I kissed you?"

"No," she said.

I put my left hand on her waist, pulled her towards me lightly, and kissed her. All the tension of the previous six months was gone. I walked her out to her car.

Her name was Ilene Myers. A year later, after many late night sessions during which we both worked on issues of the magazine, she became my wife and the essential ingredient I needed to ensure the success of *Backwoods Home Magazine*.

It was the greatest fishing trip of my life.

Freedom

The Government gorilla in our home

(originally published in September 2006)

The other week, Vince, a contractor who does occasional work for me, was arrested for slapping his 14-year-old daughter on the behind when she talked back to her mother using abusive and obscene language. Vince left a mark on his daughter's behind, enough for the local child welfare bureaucrats to accuse him of child abuse and demand he leave his home so his children would be safe. Or, they warned, he would go to jail immediately.

Vince protested that the mark he left was inadvertent and that his daughter needed a father's discipline because she was beginning to hang out with unsavory kids who were experimenting with drugs. Vince's pleas were dismissed and he was banished to an old trailer in the backyard of his home. The triumphant daughter became even more abusive to her mom, then ran away from home. She began using drugs and subsequently became pregnant.

The welfare agency made little effort to help the daughter, but the Government prosecuted Vince. He was convicted, fined, and ordered to undergo 15 months of anger management training. Vince, by the way, had no previous history of child abuse or any criminal record. His daughter is still a runaway, but Vince is not allowed near her.

Vince's predicament is not an isolated case. Many of you read-ing this story no doubt viewed the TV documentary of a few weeks ago in which a TV camera crew followed a child welfare worker into a home where the father was accused of child abuse. The father, like Vince, had slapped his 14-year-old daughter, this time across the face because she, too, was out of control. This father also left a mark on his child—a bruise on the face.

Like Vince, the TV father protested that his daughter needed a father's discipline now more than ever. The welfare worker dis-missed his pleas and said she had consulted with her supervisor by phone and the supervisor agreed with her that all his children had to be removed from the home to protect them. The man had two other younger children.

The father and mother were astonished, and they pleaded with the welfare worker not to remove their children from their home. The TV camera occasionally caught sight of a uniformed police officer who stood silently by as the drama unfolded. He was obvi-ously the power—the Government—behind the welfare worker who had decided to remove the children. Eventually, the father beseeched the welfare worker through his tears: "Don't take my children; put me in jail instead."

To no avail! Even as one child, about three years old, clung to the father and cried, "I want to stay with Daddy," the third child was awakened from his sleep from a bedroom upstairs. The wel-fare worker took the children.

The TV documentary followed the family for two years. The children were put in foster care for three months before being allowed back home. The parents eventually divorced, citing the invasion by the child welfare agency into their home as "the beginning of the end."

The documentary made no attempt to take sides with either the family or the child welfare agency, but just recorded what was happening. Call me prejudiced, but I sided with the family. I was sickened by the display of omnipotent Government bureaucratic power that seemed bent on destroying the family to save the children from a father's discipline. No wonder the parents divorced.

The program closed with a commentator stating that the debate continues as to whether Government does more harm than good when it takes a child from the home to protect it. I can't imagine many viewers went away from that program thinking that the Government did any good.

At his court hearing, my friend Vince asked the judge, "May I speak point blank or should I watch what I say?"

"You may speak point blank," the judge said.

"This system," Vince said, with his voice beginning to shake," is totally f___d up. I'm all for protecting children from abuse, but my daughter needs guidance. You're tying my hands and threatening me with jail if I go near her. What the f__k is going on?"

"Court adjourned!" the judge said and got up and left.

Court adjourned! Sounds like the pronouncement I would expect from a misguided, out-of-control Government that has given power to a gigantic and misguided, out-of-control welfare bureaucracy. We've let a big gorilla into our home to protect our children. How will we ever get it out?

Flag burning & sobriety checks

(originally published in July 1990)

There are always crackpots around who like to do things that infuriate the rest of us. Flag burners infuriate some of us so much that many otherwise clear-thinking Americans are ready to back a constitutional amendment to outlaw flag burning.

I suppose that if such a constitutional amendment passes, the flag burners will turn to burning copies of the Constitution itself. Then, I guess Congress will have to pass another constitutional amendment to outlaw that. Then the nuts will probably turn to something else, and it will go on and on until Congress just leaves the Constitution wide open so they'll be ready to counter anyone who tries to deface the symbols of our freedom.

To me, that seems to be a dangerous way to stop flag burning. Our Constitution has done pretty well for us when left alone. I can see maybe opening it up to give some oppressed minority the right to vote, but to open it up to stop a few nuts from burning the flag? Give me a break.

Why not just ignore them? Nuts always go away unless their cause has some merit. Flag burning has no merit in this country. It probably had plenty of merit in a place like Nazi Germany, but Hitler had passed a law against any kind of flag desecration. He knew it was an idea that might catch on there.

124

But America is a different story. We are the land of freedom, including freedom of speech. We tolerate the views of others, even the views of crackpots and malcontents. That's what we are all about—toleration for all sorts of views. That's what gives us such diversity and strength as a nation. A case in point is that when the founding fathers pondered making freedom of religion a right and someone pointed out it made atheism legal, Jefferson said, "Without guarding the right to be an atheist, freedom of religion is a mockery."

I would never burn the American flag, but I have no problem tolerating people who do. They're entitled to their opinion. A constitutional amendment prohibiting them from expressing their opinion, or prohibiting anyone else from expressing their opinion on any subject, does more harm to the freedoms that flag represents than all the flag burners together could ever do.

Sobriety checks

Rather than use sobriety checks to catch drunk drivers, why not surgically implant a monitor on everyone at birth to make sure no one ever drives drunk, takes drugs, cheats on their taxes, or spits on the sidewalk?

Drunk drivers should be stopped, but it should be done without the random stopping of citizens. The random stopping of civilians for any reason is wrong. If we can stop civilians today for one perceived "good reason," namely to catch drunks, we'll stop them tomorrow for another perceived "good reason," maybe to catch political dissenters.

The random stopping of civilians is a major tactic tyrannical governments have used throughout the ages to control their civilian populations. That's why our founding fathers forbade it. They were all refugees from tyrannical governments.

It's not the drunk driver we have to fear most, but Government using the drunk driver issue as an excuse to invade our private lives.

If we allow random sobriety checks to become widespread, the next thing the Government may want to do is to battle the cocaine problem by randomly searching our homes. It is an easy road to invite Government into our lives to solve the "perceived" threats to society, but it is a hard road back to the individual freedoms we Americans take for granted.

Ask some of those people lifting the yoke of Communism from their shoulders what they think of the random stopping of civilians. They'll look at you incredulously and ask, "Why do you want to do that? That's what we're trying to get away from."

Millennium excuses and the quest for truth

(originally published in November 1999)

It's time to roll out the millennium excuses to explain why society hasn't collapsed as the result of the Y2K computer bug. I know I'm a couple of months early, but January 1 will be too late to make predictions of why we haven't succumbed to Y2K doom. So here's my list of what the excuses will be. Take your choice:

Predictions for January 1:

• Society has collapsed, but the Government is covering it up. Thousands are dead or starving, but it's such a clever coverup, it'll be years before we know the staggering toll.

• We calculated the date wrong so the collapse has been postponed six months to a year. Lucky for us because we've still got a lot of food storage supplies we need to sell.

• What are you talking about? I never said society would collapse. I knew all along that nothing would happen.

• And, of course, as the usual day-to-day disasters around the world do occur, the Y2K diehards will claim that every little disaster that makes the newspaper is due to Y2K.

Predictions for January 2:

• Most doomsayers will find a new horse to ride, such as the planets lining up in one quadrant in the sky, or the impending visit by a close-encounter asteroid in 2028.

• Some government bureaucrat, maybe even Clinton, will take credit for averting the Y2K crisis, saying the Government needs broad new power over computer technology to continue averting such crises in the future.

• Russia will ask the U.S. and the I.M.F. for big new loans because they'll claim Y2K devastated their already devastated economy. They'll get the money.

Predictions for January 3:

• People who drew some money out of their bank "just in case" will begin putting it back, denying they ever thought there'd be a problem.

• The U.S. stock market will go up 250 points.

• At your local coffee bar, there will be very little talk of Y2K. It will be an embarrassing subject.

But all the concern about Y2K during the last year hasn't been a total waste of time. It's caused a mini boom in many sectors of the American economy. My subscriptions are up nicely, and once we get subscribers here we keep them with all kinds of incentives such as inexpensive anthologies and a magazine that is just too good, accurate, and honest to put down. A lot of other self-reliant businesses who have experienced significantly increased sales will have to put up with slow sales for awhile due to a glut on the market. I'm sure they are having sales meetings right now trying to identify a new doomsday scenario that needs promoting.

Have people learned anything from all the Y2K hysteria? The promoters of doom have, that's for sure. Never again will they ride a doomsday horse that has too many dates that were supposed to trigger the beginning of chaos. April 1, April 9, July 1, September 9, and October 1 were all trigger dates that came and went without Y2K incident. But I'm not sure the rest of the public has learned much. It's too much fun to get worked up about impending doom, making plans to avert it, and scaring your neighbors.

The whole experience has been dismaying to me. In an industry dominated by people who value American traditional values such as those embodied in the United States Constitution, it has been too easy for people to get distracted by phony "doom-and-gloom" scenarios such as this Y2K bug. Instead of zeroing in on what America's real problem is, namely, the declining state of freedom in this country, too many people spent all their energy on a phony Y2K crisis. Instead of concentrating on saving America, they concentrated on saving themselves from an imaginary enemy. If I had been an emerging tyrannical government trying to dissipate the angry passions of a people growing increasingly less free, I might have invented the Y2K crisis and would consider inventing many others just like it.

So being the Libertarian I am, and cherishing the freedoms enshrined in the U.S. Constitution the way I do, I thought I'd try my best to persuade people that Y2K-type crises are not our real enemies. And since you can only persuade people through knowledge, I thought the best way to persuade is by increasing people's knowledge about real things, such as real science, not the pseudoscience that accompanied the Y2K predictions of doom. So, starting with this issue, we are launching expanded homeschooling articles in the areas of science, mathematics, history, and economics in hopes of giving people a better framework from which to consider future doom-and-gloom scenarios like the Y2K crisis. If people can ward off bogus monsters, they'll have more time to battle the real monsters, like our emerging tyrannical Government.

Self-reliant people, such as those who read this magazine, are the main soldiers in the battle to retain and restore America's constitutional freedoms. America needs these people, undistracted by phony crises, to help save America and her wonderful institutions of freedom and individual liberty. If our expanded homeschooling articles can help self-reliant people tell the difference between fiction and fact, we'll feel part of the huge battle that lies ahead.

For although this country was never on the edge of a Y2K doomsday, it is on the edge of a political doomsday. And if more of us don't get our heads straight and concentrate on the real enemy at hand, namely, our own Government, America is going to become a 200-year bleap of freedom in the long history of tyranny that has reigned over people for all past millenniums.

Should both drugs and guns be legal?

(originally published in September 1999)

Answering the question of "Should drugs be legal?" is like answering the question of "Should guns be legal?" Whoever answers either question steps onto a minefield of passionate opposition—from conservatives if you say yes to drugs, and from liberals if you say yes to guns. That's why it's easier to recognize that both questions are really part of a much larger and more important question: Should government be controlled? And the answer to that question, as well as the other two, is yes.

The illegalization of drugs gives government the excuse to trample our rights, under the guise of protecting us and our children from their effects, and the illegalization of guns will give government the ability to totally trample our rights because we would have no defense against it.

What has the illegalization of drugs accomplished?

• Prisons are overcrowded with drug offenders sentenced under mandatory sentencing laws while violent offenders go free to make room. The result is the U.S. now has the highest incarceration rate in the world, made up mainly of people who have never committed a violent crime—pretty incredible for a "free" country.

• There is increased corruption in our police and judicial systems due to the large amount of money available for payoffs. The poorer you are the more likely you are to go to jail; monied drug lords with their high-priced lawyers have little to fear from the law.

• Millions of Americans who suffer from chronic pain go under-medicated because doctors are afraid to prescribe pain killers for fear of being investigated (a number have already been sent to prison) by a drug enforcement agency. A U.S. health agency has called the suffering of these patients a national disgrace.

• Seizure of property from citizens who have not been found guilty of any crime has gone sky-high, thanks to drug laws that give police the power to seize property suspected of being involved in a crime. It's up to the owner to prove his property is innocent. Orwellian?

• The War on Drugs is a repeat of Prohibition in the '30s. The amount of drugs consumed in America has not gone down appreciably, but the price of them has gone way up, making them even more attractive to sell.

What will the illegalization of guns accomplish?

• This is the classic history lesson of our century. Like all the Communist and Fascist states that outlawed guns before turning against their own people, we will be powerless to resist our government should it turn against us. And judging from our government's conduct in its War on Drugs, it already has.

What about the arguments against making drugs legal and keeping guns legal? Both are essentially the same: Drugs and guns lead to the destruction of our children, the former through destroying their physical and mental well being and the latter through killing them outright.

Both arguments play on the public's desire to protect their children at all costs. Those who would keep drugs illegal would imprison our children rather than have them take drugs, and those who would make guns illegal would expose our children to the potential enslavement of a government turned tyrannical rather than let them be endangered by guns. (Another story is the fact that Justice Department statistics show that guns are used by private citizens to prevent violent crimes far more often than they are used to commit crimes, but the stories behind those statistics never make it into the newspapers. I wonder why?)

People in government, especially the cadre of bureaucrats who think they know best how we should run our lives, find these excuses convenient to hide behind. The illegalization of drugs has given our government the excuse it needs to stop us on the street and make a warrantless search of our person, to invade our home on the suspicion we may be using drugs, and to send our children to prison for their own good. The illegalization of guns would allow the government to go even further because we would have no way to resist police in what appears to be our emerging police state.

I am the father of four children and here's what I think of the government and their conservative and liberal supporters who want to protect my children against drugs and guns: Leave my children alone. They are my concern, not yours. I would rather they ran the risk of experimenting with drugs than have some government agent send them to prison to be gang raped by hardcore criminals. And I would rather they risked being gunshot than have them live out their lives as servants to a tyrannical government without any chance to restore their freedom through armed resistance.

Drugs and guns may be bad if used badly, but an all-powerful Government is much worse. The illegalization of drugs may have sounded like a good idea in theory once, but it has given Government far too much power over us. And the proposed illegalization of guns may sound like a good idea in theory to some because it is supposed to help keep our children safe, but in reality it will take away our last and ultimate defense against government. And like our Founding Fathers, I would rather live free with some peril than live as the protected slave of government.

The question is this: Do we want a powerful government that can come into our homes or stop us on the street at will and arrest us on the suspicion we may be guilty of a crime, that can seize our property on the suspicion it is guilty, and that sends our children to prison for their own good? Or do we want a government that dares not trample on our rights guaranteed in our Constitution?

If the latter, then both drugs and guns must be legal.

The militia movement

(originally published in July 1997)

In a recent issue of *U.S. News and World Report*—a news magazine I had thought was more objective than liberal-leaning magazines like *Time* and *Newsweek*—there appeared a major article titled "Mainstreaming the militia." Far from being the objective piece I had hoped for, it was yet another distorted mainstream media reporting about the goings-on of America's mushrooming militia movement.

The article painted militia groups and other anti-government groups as being composed of unemployed, low-income, uneducated, paranoid, and easily led misfits who are seeking to blame someone—the U.S. Government, the United Nations, the New World Order, or whatever——for their troubles. *Backwoods Home Magazine* was mentioned as one of the "magazines that have sprung up to compete for the antiestablishment audience."

The article has all kinds of references to the Oklahoma City bombing, potential violence by militia groups to revenge the Waco massacre or to mark the anniversary of the Oklahoma City bombing, and the suspicion by federal agents that the militia groups are planning all sorts of violence just as an outlet for their hate and extremism.

The supposed "sources" for the information in the article comes from groups, publications, and internet sites with explosively ominous names like Klanwatch, Center on Hate and Extremism, the Hate Directory, the Program for the Study of Violence and Conflict, Skinheads USA, the Ku Klux Klan Home Page, Library of a White Tribalist, and Aryan Nations. And, of course, the books and videos these outfits sell have titles like *Hitman*, *How to Kill*, and *Ultimate Sniper* to "help Americans preparing for a race war," among other dastardly things. And, of course, these dangerous nuts all hang out at the "notorious" Preparedness Shows that are popping up all over the country.

Now, let me qualify my annoyance with this distorted and misleading *U.S.News* article by saying that neither I, my staff, nor *Backwoods Home Magazine* have membership in any militia group or other anti-government group. This is not intended as a statement to back away from these people in any way, but as an assertion that we are an independent publication that is interested in the fair treatment of all Americans, be they militia groups from America's political right or environmental groups from America's political left.

That said, I can tell you during the eight years of *BHM's* existence, I have met many militia members at the various Preparedness Shows I have attended, and I have met many environmentalists at the various environmental and energy shows I have attended. The most prominent of these people, such as John Trochmann (pictured prominently and ominously in the *U.S. News* article as the head of the "notorious" Montana Militia), and John Schaeffer (always displayed favorably in the media as the environmentally aware owner of Real Goods Corporation), are exceptionally smart businessmen and exceptionally good family men. As with other prominent people on both the left and the right, they have their hangers-on who are jerks.

What angers me, being Libertarian and conservative, is that I have never, in eight years of attending these shows in cities from Boston to Denver to Los Angeles, read anything in the mainstream media that was negative about environmental shows, or that was positive about Preparedness Shows. Even though, in my observations, the environmental shows are full of environmental crackpots, many of whom would be willing to resort to violence to promote their agenda (remember the Unabomber and tree spikers?), and the Preparedness Shows, though plagued by their own share of crackpots, by and large are attended by well-educated, well-informed, sensible people whose chief sin seems to be demanding the government behave in accordance with the Constitution.

So, why the difference in press coverage? In a nutshell: The environmental shows are full of liberals who want to promote government intervention to save the world as they think it should be, and the Preparedness Shows are full of conservatives and Libertarians who want to limit government intervention so as to save America the way they think it should be. If you are liberal, you get good press; if not, you get tagged as a racist, extremist, or nutcase. It just makes me so mad I could spit.

Well, at least the *U.S. News* article was partly right when it said the militia movement is becoming more mainstream, but it underestimates the appeal. Instead of the six Preparedness Expos it said are planned for this year, there are at least 19. They are in cities like Orlando, Portland, Indianapolis, Phoenix, Kansas City, San Francisco, Albuquerque, San Antonio, Nashville, Tulsa, Detroit,

Philadelphia, Pittsburgh, Buffalo, St. Louis, Columbus, San Diego, and Dallas. Some have already taken place.

You see, *U.S. News*, Americans aren't really influenced by how much you or the rest of the mainstream media distort the meaning of a legitimate American movement. They've been down this freedom road before. And what the militia movement is in America is a healthy exercise of freedom—what freedoms we have left—to oppose the excesses of our own government. If it has racists and extremists on its fringes, so does every other movement this country has ever had. You concentrate on the fringes to pull off your distortion, but big government zealots like you have never been able to stamp out the real truth with your high-profile distortions.

The *U.S. News* article is right about one thing, and I'll quote it: "...the mainstreaming of the militia movement has just begun."

Postscript: The last sentence of this article proved inaccurate. Then Attorney General Janet Reno came down hard on militias across the country, with the FBI infiltrating many and the Government putting militia members on trial for various types of conspiracies to commit violence. The 40-year prison sentences meted out to some militia members, most of whom were people with no criminal record, but who owned guns and liked to talk tough at militia meetings about how they would take action against Government, quickly snuffed out the budding interest in militias. The Preparedness Shows, likewise, went extinct.

Thanks for not killing them

(originally published in November 1997)

We're entering the season when traditionally we express our thanks to someone, often the Almighty, for something we feel fortunate in having, such as our fine family, our health, or perhaps just our turkey dinner. I've broadened my thankfulness this year to include the federal government, the Oregon National Guard, the Oregon State Police, the Salem (Oregon) SWAT team, and the Marion County (Oregon) Sheriff's Department.

I'm thankful to them for not killing some friends of mine, namely Paul Revere, founder of Embassy of Heaven Church, located in Marion County, Oregon, his lovely wife, Rachel, and their two charming daughters, Brooke, age 17, and Skye, age 14. The stage was certainly set for these police agencies to do so earlier this year. Just after dawn one January morning, dark-clad members of these agencies, equipped with an armored vehicle and carrying an assortment of automatic weapons, raided the church, breaking down doors, smashing windows, ordering the family and several other members of the church out of bed, and carrying Revere and other church members off to jail. After some desperate pleading from Rachel, they allowed the petrified daughters to stay in her care. At the jail, one of Revere's fingers was broken as he was forcibly fingerprinted.

The Revere family's crime was that they had failed to pay their property taxes, and Marion County officials, backed up by the law (the county had denied the church's request for tax-exempt status) and urged on by county officials who had demonized the church and its members as dangerous extremists, had orchestrated the raid to seize and confiscate the 34-acre church property for nonpayment of $16,000 in taxes. The property had been valued at $119,000.

When I read of the raid I was deeply troubled and reminded of the bungled police raids at Ruby Ridge in Idaho during which the FBI managed to kill Randy Weaver's wife and son, and at Waco, Texas, during which 80 people, many of them children, were incinerated in a fire. I was troubled but grateful that the police had acted with enough restraint not to cause the death of any member of the Revere family or their church.

It struck me as absurd, but a sign of our tragic times, that I had to worry about friends of mine being killed by their own government. And I found it equally tragic that most of the newspaper and media accounts of the raid were sympathetic to the government agencies, not the Revere family. The Revere family and its church were, according to news accounts, extremists—and that modern-day buzz word made them eligible for persecution, even death, at the hands of the government. What a disturbing world we live in when the United States of America, of all countries, could so easily justify such a view.

I had come to know the Revere family at the various Preparedness Expos they had attended to spread their interpretation of the Bible. Revere, with wild beard and hair, certainly looked different from the clean-cut TV evangelist, or the well-groomed priest or minister. But rather than the hand-waving, impassioned preacher, he was a calm, considerate man who talked to whoever came up to his vendor's booth. Put simply, he believed in the Kingdom of Heaven and thought mankind owed allegiance only to that kingdom, and that we had no obligation to abide by the rules of any kingdom or government of this earth. His Embassy of Heaven Church had its own government. Revere refused to pay taxes of any kind, or even to apply to the government for a driver's license. Instead his church issued its own driver's licenses. Many of us at the Preparedness Shows thought Revere's beliefs peculiar, but not dangerous. He did not believe in violence and saw no use for firearms.

His daughters added a touch of refinement and elegance to the shows. Meticulously clad in long, flowing dresses, the beautiful and always smiling young ladies sold pencil-shaped packets of honey for a dollar as part of their effort to help their father's church. My daughter, Annie, whose age falls between that of the two girls, often joined them in tours of the aisles. The other vendors were always glad to see them; they brought gaiety and charm to the sometimes somber political mood of the shows.

When I saw Revere and his family at our most recent Preparedness Show, I greeted them with a much bigger than usual smile, because I knew I was lucky to have had the chance to greet them at all after their encounter with one of today's most dangerous entities—government. During the three-day show they did as they had done at previous shows: Shared their homemade stews and cookies with me, tended my booth while I went off to conduct business with other show vendors, and generally made my stay at the show more pleasant. They have never tried to convert me to their beliefs, perhaps realizing I was beyond conversion to anything. And as at previous shows, they never asked for anything in return.

The Revere family has been homeless since that January raid. They have lived in a couple of trailers donated to them, on some land owned by a man they had ministered to while he was in prison. For this show, they were camped out at a friend's property. They are trying to get their former property back, but I am not hopeful for them. Revere still has that calm and composed defiance against worldly governments; if the governments who raided his church and took his property thought they broke Revere's spirit, they are wrong.

But the government has had the last say, in a worldly way, and these "extremists" have been put in their place. But at least, this time, the government didn't kill them. And for that, I guess I should say thanks.

Postscript: The Revere family never did get their property back. Their Embassy of Heaven Church (www.embassyofheaven.com), however, is still going strong.

The beast is at the door again

(originally published in July 1994)

As our important holidays like July 4 approach, it forces many of us to reflect on the freedoms the people of America still enjoy, but it also makes us look sadly upon the freedoms we have lost. We are still the most free country ever, but our freedoms have been gradually eroded since the time those enlightened men drafted that great doctrine that protects us from Government: The Constitution.

Notice I said protects us from Government. Today all the talk is protecting us from crime, from drugs, from AIDS, from guns, and from—you name it—everything from inadequate health care to second-hand smoke.

But those framers of so long ago never had any intention of protecting us from things like second-hand smoke. They knew who the real enemy was. They were students of history, and they understood that the great evil that had stalked mankind throughout the ages had not been plagues or criminals or even invading armies. It was a people's own Government, which had always been more master than protector.

That's why men like Thomas Jefferson and James Madison and the rest of our founding fathers are so revered. They solved mankind's most ancient and critical dilemma by figuring out how

143

to keep Government at bay and guaranteeing lasting freedom to the people. They did it with a carefully worded document that placed all power with the people and allocated only certain powers to the Government. It wasn't a perfect document, but it was close.

But, as many of us have sadly come to realize in this modern era, Government is back. In an effort to respond to various groups' demands that "the people" be "protected" from the many plagues that afflict modern society, Government has gleefully responded.

Here's a short, incomplete list:

To respond to crime, Government has built prisons so that the United States now has the highest per-capita incarceration rate in the world, much higher than much maligned, second-place South Africa.

To respond to drug abuse, Government has waged a war on drugs that has included "no-knock" laws, seizure of private property without due process, and massive corruption of public officials.

To respond to AIDS, Government has decided that public schools will give our children condoms and sex instruction without the consent or approval of parents.

To combat inadequate health care, Government is attempting to institute socialized medicine, along with what it says is a central computer databank with records on not just our medical needs, but on every aspect of our personal and monetary status.

To combat guns, Government is passing new restrictive gun laws against guns (they call them assault rifles) that are seldom used in crimes, and they want to register all gun owners. Their intention clearly is to confiscate all guns, the second Amendment be damned.

Everyone remembers the Government's two most recent and notorious attempts to control guns. One was at Ruby Ridge in Idaho and the other near Waco, Texas.

In Idaho, undercover Government agents convinced Randy Weaver to sell them an illegal gun. We used to call that entrapment, but now the Government calls it an excuse to invade an individual's home. The Government invaded Weaver's home, shot his wife through the head, his 14-year-old son in the back, and put Weaver on trial. Weaver was acquitted, but his wife and son are still dead.

Near Waco, Texas, the Government went after guns at the Branch Davidian compound. I won't recount the horrible details, but we all saw the fire that killed 86 people, about half of them innocent women and children. The survivors were put on trial, but were acquitted of any serious charges.

And the Government has just begun. It intends to go much further.

In an effort to combat what Government fears is too much criticism, mainly by the hundreds of small conservative talk shows that have cropped up across the country to criticize Government erosion of our constitutional rights, Government, under the guise of a misnamed law called the "Fairness Doctrine," is actively considering regulating radio to allow "opposing" views to be aired.

Sounds scary?

As it has always done, somehow Government, like some monster from the past, has again outwitted the freedom-loving masses and has convinced them that they don't need protection from

Government, but from everything else. And so the age-old beast our founding fathers had tamed is once more banging at our door.

It's a frightening prospect that it will get inside our homes again because it may take hundreds of years before enlightened men like Jefferson and Madison come along again to rescue us.

Countdown to freedom's Armageddon

(originally published in January 1999)

As the one-year countdown to the year 2000 commences, like many of you, I am preparing myself and my family for potential disruptions in food, electrical, water, medical, and other supplies. I am doing it in spite of the fact that I do not believe the Millennium Bug, the computer date problem that many say has the potential to cause a widespread collapse in our society's computer-dependent delivery systems, will cause as much damage as the doomsayers predict. However, the risk is significant enough that I am taking no chances with my family. Also, the risk that the world economic collapse will hit America is also great enough for me to act.

Luckily, my home is pretty self-sufficient because I practice self-reliance. I am far away from a city, have my own water source and purification system, good wood heat system, a pantry loaded with food and essential supplies, and have enough guns and ammo to handle most anything. To supplement this, I am installing a photovoltaic system at my home for electricity, am increasing the size of my pantry, and am acquiring medical necessities and knowledge, among other things. I'm also getting my boat up to snuff since I live next to a great food source—the Pacific Ocean.

However, I am still worried. Not that I won't be prepared for whatever physical dangers might threaten my family, but for the political dangers that threaten them. Because the political dangers are the only likely long-term catastrophes my family and yours will experience from the onset of the millennium. Even if other problems materialize, they will be of a relatively short duration, but the political dangers, such as a major loss of freedom because the government decides to step in and "help us," will, if history is an indicator, be a long-term disaster. Political disasters, such as a major loss of freedom, tend to take generations to recover from, if ever.

That's why it's important for all of us to think about our freedom, and the tentative hold we have on it, at the same time we are planning for our physical safety for the coming millennium.

Consider the last big loss-of-freedom event in our history: The Great Depression of 1929. People gladly gave up many basic freedoms to government in hopes the government would save them. World War II saved them, but the freedoms the government took are still gone in the form of the massive welfare society we have today in which government takes, on average, 40% of our income and transfers it to someone else, and in the form of the regulatory nightmare we all live in.

What freedoms will government try and take this time? Will it use the millennium panic to clamp down on the internet, which I believe is the most significant freedom tool in centuries, equal to the invention of the printing press? I think that's a good possibility, since government wants desperately to control the internet, and since most of us are too busy protecting ourselves against computers to be bothered about saving them. Or will it make a grab for something else?

Freedom, and the tools that make freedom possible, cannot afford many great losses. The people of America got freedom about 200 years ago, and ever since they've been letting it slip away, primarily because they've been preoccupied with protecting themselves against other perceived physical dangers. Each year, politicians convince enough voters that we need new laws to protect us against something or other, and so we heap freedom-restricting laws and regulations on ourselves. Would we were as vigilant against these sinister, freedom-robbing laws as we have been against this Millennium Bug.

Does anyone remember Patrick Henry? In the early days of our country, while we were still fighting for our freedoms, he said, "Give me liberty or give me death!" That's how important freedom was to a person on the verge of securing it, in an era when few people had it. Physical safety was barely a contender in importance.

Perhaps we should consider what freedom is in the midst of our struggle for physical safety in the new millennium. Freedom is the philosophical idea put into practice by the American Revolution that holds that a person who is willing to be responsible for himself has a right to run his own life, in whatever way he pleases, so long as he doesn't harm others. Government has no say, but acts only as a policeman to prevent domestic and foreign aggression.

It took several millennia—since the time of Aristotle—to develop this idea, and many people including American patriots who fought off a powerful British army more than 200 years ago, gave up their physical comfort and their lives to achieve it. People prior to the American Revolution had lived under one secular and religious tyranny after another; notions of people free to pursue

149

their own happiness and protected under the umbrella of freedom were ruthlessly crushed, just as King George tried to crush the American Revolution.

The American Revolution, with its philosophy of freedom for the individual, became the greatest political achievement in the history of mankind. And with this achievement, mankind's spirit was set free to achieve our modern civilization with all its labor-saving conveniences.

So while you and I prepare ourselves for the physical dangers that may accompany the onset of the new millennium, let's be at least as vigilant against the real danger that lies ahead: That government will make another major grab for our most valuable possession—our freedom.

New World Order — old world stench!

(originally published in May 1992)

Here's the main front-page headline of the *Los Angeles Times* newspaper on a recent morning:

World Leaders Urge U.N. to Safeguard Rights Everywhere

The article beneath it described a summit gathering of world leaders at the United Nations at which most of the major powers called on the U.N. to expand its role and move to "protect human rights everywhere in the world."

French President Francois Mitterand even called for the establishment of a permanent U.N. military force that could be dispatched to enforce U.N. decisions. Besides Mitterand, the meeting included all the big U.N. guns: U.S. President George Bush, British Prime Minister John Major, Russian President Boris Yeltsin (assuming the former Soviet seat), and Chinese Premier Li Peng, who was the lone dissenting voice.

Even Japanese Prime Minister Kiichi Miyazawa was there saying he expected Japan will be given veto power at the U.N. by 1995 since it will be expected to foot the bill for these U.N. adventures. Japan's former World War II ally, Germany, was also there, predicting it, too, would soon enjoy veto power at the U.N.

Someone pinch me. Am I living a soap opera or a nightmare? It's hard to tell whether to laugh or cry. The "morally correct" bosses at the U.N., still feeling jubilant and righteous a year after their victory over Iraq in their first "world policing" action, now want to clean up the rest of the world in accordance with their views of who is morally correct and who is morally wrong.

Is this what President Bush had in mind when he kept referring to The New World Order during the Iraq War? Is this the beginning of World Government, or a transitional step to it? By gosh, I think that's exactly what these leaders hope it is.

So, why aren't the people in the streets protesting? Are we all asleep? Didn't East Bloc Communism with all its Big Government totalitarianism just crumble under its own misguided weight? Didn't Democracy just triumph in country after country? Weren't we just celebrating the victory of individual freedom over state totalitarianism? Or was all that just a pleasant dream?

Are we now back to the nightmare of reality? Big Government with all its trampling on individual freedom is not dying after all. It has merely regrouped and is, in fact, on the rise in the form of The New World Order, in the shape of what these world leaders at the U.N. hope is the beginning of World Government.

We, as free people, should be shaking in our boots. These are not boasting flunkies like Hussein; these are the most powerful politicians on the planet. And much of the mass media is treating their suggestions like they're pretty good ideas, like they may even be the inevitable evolution of government. These world leaders, with the help of an applauding media and our own lethargy, could well pull off World Government in the midst of what we thought was a world triumph of individual freedom.

And they are not even being very original how they do it. Moral excuses like "protecting human rights" have always been used to justify the increase of government power. It sounds good! Who would object? Certainly not a mass media that believes strongly in Big Government.

But examine the history of the U.S.; ever since our founding fathers laid ink to that special parchment we call our Bill of Rights, Big Government "do-gooders" have been chipping away at our individual freedoms in the name of "protecting the human rights" of someone or other. Trouble is, every time someone's human rights got protected, our personal freedoms got diminished.

That's how the old Soviet Union grew to be so big. They wanted to protect the rights of workers. The Soviet Union didn't collapse because the Communists lost their zeal for their cause; they simply ran out of money.

The zealots in the West who still see Big Government as the way of the future have not lost their zeal for the cause, either. Despite Communism's fall, they still think all of societies' problems can be solved by Big Government forcing solutions down the throats of all of us. This World Government idea is right up their alley. It's a big hammer that will be used to smash individual freedoms in the name of "protecting human rights" somewhere around the globe, or somewhere in our own country.

I thought the demise of Communism around the world would give us a reprieve from Big Government. But instead of a reprieve, the powerful politicians in the West see an opening for even bigger government—their style of "morally correct" Big World Government.

Talk about nightmares: Old World War II enemies and old Cold War enemies all together in one Big World Government. And Japan the banker! George Orwell should be here to see this. It's his story.

Is it time for an education revolution?

(originally published in September 2002)

Education is important, right? Of course it is. Then college must be really important, right? ... Did I hear some of you pause before saying, "Well, yeah, I guess so."

If so, you may have come to the same conclusion I have—that college these days is a very iffy proposition. Not because it's expensive, but because, for most of the degrees it confers, it has little to do with education but much to do with instilling "politically correct" thinking into the minds of its students.

Except for the sciences and some business courses, college is pretty much a waste of time today for people who want to be truly educated. Most higher education, and virtually all primary public education, has become the tool of choice for liberals desperate to maintain and expand their power in America by capturing the minds of our youth. Sound far fetched? Let me give you an historical example of what I'm talking about.

At the dawn of the 17th century, the Roman Catholic Church had a near monopoly on the university system in the Western World, just as the liberal political establishment does today. In the 17th century, the Church taught that important knowledge was handed down by the Church, with the Pope as the final arbiter of what was true and what was false. Inquiry was pursued within the framework of Aristotelian cause-and-effect argument, but the Church's precepts were not to be questioned. Among those precepts was that the earth stood at the center of the universe. Galileo, the greatest scientist of his age, was imprisoned for supporting the Copernican assertion that the earth really orbited the sun. To the church and educational leadership of the day, truth was less important than dogma.

Developments in astronomy and technology, which included the invention of the telescope, which was invented outside of the university system, proved Galileo right, of course, while other discoveries showed the university system to be wrong about many things. But it took a mighty intellectual struggle that lasted into the 18th century to wrest control of the universities, and hence the intellectual development of the bulk of mankind, away from the ecclesiastics. Many of the discoveries and inventions that ushered in our modern age took place outside the university system in private societies and clubs that formed as an alternative for people who wanted intellectual freedom. The fruits of these clubs included the scientific method and the discoveries of magnetism, electricity, and the laws of the cosmos. As 17th century universities contemplated the number of angels that could sit on the head of a pin, the societies and clubs discovered the nature of the world. They not only invented our modern world, but their passion for seeking the truth in all things, including political systems, led directly to the greatest political achievement of all time, the U.S. Constitution and its Bill of Rights.

Now we seem to find ourselves back at square one. The liberal establishment with its politically correct ideas of wealth redistribution, the evils of capitalism, and the sanctity of causes like global warming, animal rights, and all sorts of other nonsense founded on nothing more than their "feel-good" ideology, now controls the universities and is teaching their phony philosophy to our children. It's not much different than the 17th century Church teaching false precepts to their students.

The pressure to attend college these days is tremendous. If you can ingest the politically correct liberal line for four years, you get your ticket to employment, your diploma. That piece of paper is good for a job in our government's giant bureaucracy, the military's officer ranks, and a variety of big corporations. Even police agencies now require a degree to become a cop.

Most parents believe their children must go to college "to succeed." That was true as well when the ecclesiastics held power in the 17th century universities. And if, by success, we mean getting a good job with a big corporation, then I guess it is true. But is that really all we want for ourselves and our children? Do we really want our children to settle for a life of mindless adherence to corporate and government bosses?

If so, today's colleges and universities are doing a great job. Our children will become experts at adhering to the modern liberal dogma as handed down by the universities, and they will no doubt become good soldiers for whatever government or corporation they work for. It is just too bad that many of them will become incapable of any original thoughts, lest it interfere with their jobs.

I get submissions in my office all the time from wannabe experts whose resumes listing their degrees are longer and more impressive than their articles. With rare exceptions, the people I find with knowledge and ideas, and with the ability to transmit their knowledge and ideas to others, are not degreed but self-educated.

I think it's time we did what 17th and 18th century intellectuals did and find an alternative to the university system. History is a great teacher. It tells us what has worked and not worked in the past, so we can better understand what will likely work in the present and future. Sadly, today's university system ignores the lessons of the past and works primarily as a way for the ruling liberal class to maintain its power and spread its political ideology. It does a great job of everything except truly educating our youth.

Media

Old Media vs. the New Media — a battle that's good for America

Raise your hand if you think TV newscasters, radio commentators, or major newspapers report the news in a fair and balanced manner. I don't see many hands going up. I know mine's not up. I like to channel surf TV news stations to get each station's take on a given news event. The difference is stark. CNN and the networks have a marked liberal bias, while Fox News has a marked conservative bias. The difference is just as stark with other media, with major newspapers leaning heavily to the left and radio commentators and internet bloggers leaning heavily to the right. There is a very understandable reason for this, and from my perspective, it's not necessarily a bad thing.

In a nutshell, Fox News and radio commentators are part of what some conservatives like to call the New Media, while CNN, the TV networks, and major newspapers are part of the Old Media. The New Media has existed for a very short time, starting with the arrival of Rush Limbaugh on talk radio and the creation of Fox News on TV. It is still fairly small compared to the Old Media, but it has been growing in viewership and listenership for at least 10 years, in just about direct proportion to the decline in viewership and readership of the Old Media. The rise of internet bloggers, those individuals in cyberspace (the Drudge Report is only one example) who have taken it upon themselves to comment on the news on their websites, has just about sounded the death knell for the Old Media.

Bloggers are beginning to hold the Old Media to account. Just one recent example: Senator John Kerry's "bad joke" a week before the midterm elections when he seemed to insinuate that young people who don't study hard and "get smart" wind up getting "stuck in Iraq." That remark was reported on only one daytime TV news broadcast, until an internet blogger picked it up and began writing about it and posting it at various websites. Other bloggers took it from there, and with the incredible speed of the internet, millions of Americans who have become accustomed to surfing the internet began a sort of online town meeting and demanded Kerry apologize to the troops for his perceived bad joke. Other New Media outlets such as Fox News and talk radio picked it up too, of course, and the Old Media was reluctantly forced to cover the story in a major way. Kerry's "bad joke" went from obscurity to a public relations disaster for the Democratic Party in a handful of nanoseconds. Kerry ended up cancelling the remainder of his many scheduled appearances on behalf of Democratic candidates.

Most people who inhabit the Old Media, namely reporters, and many who have grown to rely on the Old Media for the information they get about the world, think the New Media is outrageously biased with a conservative agenda. Many inhabitants of the New Media, especially on talk radio, admit their bias, but they correctly claim the Old Media reporters are just as biased but try to pass their bias off as objective reporting.

I'm a former member of the Old Media, having been a reporter for several daily newspapers and written many news stories that supported the liberal slant of the papers for which I worked, and I'm a current member of the New Media, being the publisher of *Backwoods Home Magazine*, which features conservative topics like guns and contains editorials that, more often than not, promote conservative and Libertarian values. So I've gained perspective over the years about why the New Media will continue to grow and the Old Media continue to shrink until there is a balance between them.

Up until the advent of talk radio and Fox News, the Old Media had a virtual monopoly on what passed as news. Guns were bad, schools were underfunded, abortion and sexual orientation was a right, welfare was good, taxes were not a problem, and the United Nations was a terrific idea. These were just some of the things that were the dogma that found its way into newscasts, from the selection of what stories would be reported to the "play" they would be given.

This monopoly of the news worked fine for many years, except that an increasing segment of the population viewed the news they saw on TV or read in the newspaper with skepticism. It just didn't jive with the values of Americans who own about 200 million firearms that guns were the culprit every time there was a crime involving a gun, or that schools were underfunded every time a study claimed a lot of high school graduates couldn't read. So, a lot of these people were primed and ready to listen when Rush Limbaugh came along and said guns were not the culprit but criminals were, schools were not underfunded but the school system was mismanaged, and a slew of other conclusions that were not being aired by the Old Media.

Now there are many talk show hosts playing to that same audience. It's true that a few talk shows have also risen to support the

Old Media's traditional bias, but most of them cannot raise the advertising support the New Media has been able to, so must be funded by political action groups like moveon.org. That says a lot about who the listening audience is.

And Fox News is an even bigger success story. It's now the most-watched news channel in most of the TV markets where it is aired, even though it's competing against much larger Old Media news outlets such as network TV and the giant of the news airways, CNN.

This battle between the Old Media and the New Media is good old American competition. Just as politicians need to be thrown out of office for not being good stewards of the institutions that make America flourish, the news media needs to be held to account.

As a people, Americans are very good at being able to intuit an internal problem and begin acting, as a group, in a way that solves that problem. It's sort of like the public cutting back on gasoline when oil prices go up; it brings the cost of oil, and ultimately gas, back down. But the American ability to find ways to solve internal problems is far more incisive, and it extends to all areas of our society. It's an ability, I think, that is a natural outgrowth of a country that has been steeped for so long in freedom. We don't like people telling us lies, whether it's the politicians or news reporters.

What is at stake, as usual, is the future road America will travel. It's a marvelous example, I think, of why America is so successful. They are a very self-reliant people who make decisions at the individual level, resisting attempts by politicians or news reporters to guide them.

The Old Media has lost its monopoly, even though its news out-lets still vastly outnumber the New Media. But the pendulum is clearly swinging in favor of the New Media, driven by consumers who simply want to know what's really going on. This is a very good thing, even if, in the short-term, most of the New Media has a right-wing bias. That's somewhat refreshing from my view; I'm sick of the liberal slant in the news. Besides, Americans won't settle for slanted news of any kind. The pendulum will settle somewhere in the middle, giving us what we should have had all along—fair and balanced news.

The "Leave Us Alone" coalition and some alternative news sources

(originally published in September 1996)

Ever notice the way the news media and big government seem to work together, both at the national and local level?

At the national level, it's fairly obvious: If President Clinton had been anything other than the big-government Democrat he is, the media would have deep-fried him long ago over things like Whitewater, Travelgate, Filegate, Vince Foster, Paula Jones, Web Hubbel, Guy Tucker, the MacDougals, or any of his other friends who are either under indictment, on trial, or in jail. Imagine Ronald Reagan surviving a portfolio like that?

But, on the local level, the collusion is much more subtle. I picked up my local newspaper this morning and read one of the main front-page headlines: *Property tax jump unlikely.* The slightly smaller subheadline read: *Assessor says values level off.* The prominently displayed story was essentially a feel-good piece about the local tax assessor's office because he was not only *not* going to raise taxes, but he was going to lower some people's taxes a little. Wow, what a guy!

The same newspaper a week ago prominently featured a list of county services that would be cut unless voters passed two upcoming ballot tax levies. Ominously, libraries and fire services were at the top of the list. I couldn't help but link the two stories—you know, since they're giving us a break on property taxes, we should pass the two levies and save the libraries and fire stations.

But, I'm probably just paranoid. After all I'm a right-wing, knee-jerk, mean-spirited conservative who could care less about libraries and fire stations, not to mention children, old people, and anything else big government taxing and spending is meant to help.

Buried inside today's newspaper is a story I consider important: ***Taxpayers' bill passes in Senate.*** The subheadline read: ***Legislation aimed at abuses of IRS.*** The story is about legislation passed overwhelmingly by both houses of Congress to make it easier for taxpayers to sue the IRS for wrongful collection of taxes. The story termed the bill a "Taxpayer Bill of Rights" and listed all kinds of ways Americans could legally tell the IRS to take a hike. But I guess the newspaper didn't think that story very important, so it played it down by placing it inside the paper.

You know, I'm sick of the way the news media tries to feed me the news. They either ignore or play down stories I think are important, and they put on the front page news stories I often think are self-serving to their big government allies in politics. From my local newspaper to national television news, they filter it through their own narrow big-government-is-the-solution-to-everything prejudice. Did you know that more than 85% of the members of the news media admit to being liberals or Democrats? I suppose it's only natural for them to think big government is the solution to most problems. They probably can't begin to comprehend that someone like me just wants to be left alone, that I pay my property taxes grudgingly and think they should be abolished altogether, and that I think most tax levies are a waste of money, even the ones the lying (or stupid) news media claim are the only way to keep the libraries and fire stations from closing.

I am a member of that newest huge coalition that has emerged in America during the last few years—the "Leave Us Alone" coalition. We're made up of people with differing opinions, but what we share in common is we don't like big government with its tax-and-spend solutions, and we don't trust the news media, which has become little more than the mouthpiece of big government.

And as many members of the "Leave Us Alone" coalition have done, I've begun not only resisting all attempts by big government to control my life, but I've begun turning off the news media and turning to alternative methods of getting news. For example, I have cancelled my subscription to my local newspaper and have stopped listening to most national television news.

Instead, I rely on several good newsletters and radio shows, but in particular I rely on the relatively unfiltered versions of news found on TV's C-SPAN network and the comprehensive news CNN offers over the internet on its World Wide Web page. Even though CNN still arranges news selectively on the internet, it's easy to rearrange the news according to my own view of what's important, and it's easy to dig deep into a story, getting all the detail I want, even to the point of going right into a politician's e-mail basket and telling him what I think.

The internet, I think, is emerging as the greatest freedom tool of the 20th century. No wonder big government is already making noises about controlling the Internet to save—get this—the children from pornography. What a laugh. Who they really want to save is—you guessed it—themselves.

A history lesson from Ayn Rand

(originally published in March 1997)

For the past several weeks I've been reading the *Letters of Ayn Rand*, which is a collection covering her letters from 1926, when she arrived in America from Russia, to 1982, when she died. Ayn Rand is the author of, among other things, two brilliant novels called *The Fountainhead* and *Atlas Shrugged*, both of which defended American capitalism and individualism during an era in which all the rage in this country, at least among the media and academia, was the apparent success of Soviet Communism.

Her letters apply to today for two important reasons:

1) They reveal a climate in America during the 1930s and 40s when there was intense bias from the media and academia against people like Rand who supported individualism and opposed collectivism, which, in an accurate sense, is the umbrella term encompassing all the state-controlled political systems of that day, such as Communism, Fascism, Nazism, and Socialism.

2) They reveal a climate of timid opposition to collectivism by capitalists and conservatives, who Rand believed far outnumbered the collectivists who controlled the media, publishing houses, universities, and the entertainment industry. It was Rand's contention that the media, publishers, Hollywood, and academia so controlled the information Americans had access to,

169

that it created an artificial climate in which many people were cowed into thinking there was widespread approval of collectivism. And any time someone did speak up loudly for capitalism or individualism, the media of the day branded them as "capitalist exploiters," or even more effectively, the media simply didn't report their views, so few people knew these vocal opponents of collectivism even existed.

Does that sound familiar to you today, in the 1990s?

The media and company still sing the praises of collectivism, and they still have timid, scared opponents in us conservatives. They have, of course, discarded discredited terms like collectivism and Communism, since all the countries who adopted those anti-individualist philosophies have collapsed under the weight of their own bad ideas. They now ride new horses that push collectivist thinking, such as environmentalism, feminism, welfarism, etc. These are all good causes, they say, and require the federal government to tax us heavily, interfere strongly in our personal affairs, and pass hundreds of laws and impose thousands of regulations on individuals, just as the old collectivism did.

And the media and their allies, still hostile to those who think American capitalism and self-reliance are best, still deal with them in the same way they did in the 1930s—not by calling them capitalist exploiters (that term is too foolish sounding in light of capitalist success all over the world), but by calling them "right-wing extremists," "patriot haters," and "racist militia members." But still the best way the media has of dealing with these modern individualists is by ignoring them. The media perfected that technique in the 1930s and 40s. As Ayn Rand wrote in 1943 to a sympathetic company owner who had experienced labor problems: "We are not allowed to be heard and the country at large does not even know that we exist, fight and are being murdered by methods much dirtier than those used against you by the thugs of the CIO. You were facing a firing squad. We are being choked in a cellar."

Does that ring kind of true today for all you conservative groups out there who can't get your side of a story into a newspaper or on television? You bet it does.

But if the tactics of the media and their allies have not changed since the 1930s, neither has the timidity of conservatives. We have our prominent talk-show hosts, but many conservatives run from them as soon as the media begins calling them hate mongers. We are afraid we, too, might be branded a hater, even though we know that the media people who would call us haters are liars.

Maybe it's time we conservatives stood up and showed the media and their allies just how big we are. Maybe it's time we began actively supporting those conservatives who stick their neck out in the cause of individualism and against modern collectivism.

In a 1943 letter, Ayn Rand wrote: "The indifference of most of our conservative national leaders to young beginners who wish to serve our cause, has ruined us and delivered the whole intellectual field to the Reds. A new 'conservative' writer, these days, is left in the position of having his throat cut by an organized Red gang, while the leaders of his side look on, faintly bored, or turn away."

It's obvious to me that the organized Red gang is still in place. Soviet Communism may have failed after a 70-year disastrous experiment, but the Red gang is still succeeding at slitting the throats of emerging conservatives.

In a letter in 1941, Rand wrote: "If I were a defender of Communism, I'd be a Hollywood millionaire-writer by now." That's still true today. Write a book about saving the planet and the media will push it for you, get you on the Donahue show, and make you a star. Write a book about saving your country from the collectivism that destroyed the Soviet Union, and it'll never be published.

Nothing has changed. The collectivists are too stupid (or too determined) to accept the reality that their ideas are junk. They won't give up until we take the media, Hollywood, academia, and the universities back.

(If you'd like to read Ayn Rand's letters for yourself, the book was published in 1995 by Dutton, a division of Penguin Books USA, 375 Hudson St., New York, NY 10014. ISBN 0-525-93946-6, $34.95.)

The new power of the mass media is eroding the freedom of the press

(originally published in March 1993)

One of the greatest freedoms a person can have is the freedom to speak one's mind honestly and openly. It's one of the freedoms we have taken for granted in this country, and one that is being steadily eroded in a manner most of us could never have imagined.

Not that we can't still speak our mind most of the time. It's just that we don't get heard very well these days unless we say things that are politically correct to the ears of the mass media, which controls how many people hear us. Since most members of the mass media are liberals, liberal causes get more air time than conservative causes. There are many good examples. The Presidential election of '92 is an important one. The media strongly favored Clinton over Bush, so did everything it could to get Clinton elected, such as emphasizing every small bit of bad economic news, like rising unemployment and the growing federal deficit, and ignoring any good economic news. The day after Clinton got elected, the media began emphasizing only the good economic news, as if his very election miraculously turned the economy around. They seldom mention that unemployment and the federal deficit are still growing. In effect, they are lying to the people.

Anything to do with guns is always a good example. When some Koreans in L.A. successfully defended their stores against L.A. rioters, the media gave them only passing attention, but emphasized over and over the plight of the poor in our cities' ghettos and how billions in federal money was needed to set things right. That's because the liberal media hates guns, but loves big government spending to cure social ills. If someone uses a gun to defend his family, it is usually not reported at all.

Somalia is another example. The media, being a big fan of globalist ideas like World Government and an all-powerful U.N. police force to enforce human rights around the world, saw Somalia as the perfect example to show how well World Government could work. So, they bombarded us with TV pictures of starving Somali children until George Bush, the greatest backer of World Government on the planet, felt "obliged" to send in the Marines. A typical conservative view of this intervention is that it is a new form of colonialism disguised as humanitarianism and that it is merely setting the stage for unwise U.S./U.N. intervention in places like Bosnia Herzegovina, located in that part of the world where World War I was ignited. But you won't hear much of that view in the mass media.

Other examples abound. Feminist groups who still sing the praises of Anita Hill and castigate Supreme Court Justice Clarence Thomas are given all the media play they want. The media also gives ample space to the Hollywood-led boycott of Colorado because voters there voted down a proposal to give gays and lesbians special rights. And environmental pseudo-scientists who still insist that the earth's ozone layer is disappearing still get air time every time they open their mouths, even though real science has shown time and again that there is no evidence to back up their claim. Say anything in favor of Clarence Thomas, Colorado voters, or exaggerated environmental claims, and it will likely be ignored by the mass media.

That's because the liberal mass media is not in the business of informing people with objective news; they are in the business of trying to shape people's opinions by inundating them with selective slices of news that support their political agenda. Their feeling is if they bombard you with enough ozone stories, you'll come to believe the ozone is disappearing, and if they bombard you with enough anti-gun stories, you'll believe guns are evil. They got Clinton elected as our President, got us involved in Somalia, and will soon try to pass sweeping environmental legislation that will solve fictitious ecological problems.

There are few conservative publications out there to combat this one-sided reporting, but those publications are simply ignored by the mass media. Seldom are their articles and columns reprinted in the mass media, but let some liberal college rag out of Berkeley or Harvard Square put forth some screwball idea about cow farts causing the ozone layer to disappear, and the mass media will put them on the front page.

It's a damn shame. The mass media might as well be the political party that is always in power because their ability to flood the airwaves and print media with their side of the story to the exclusion of the "other" side of the story is driving most of the political decisions that are made in this country. The main reason we are traveling the fast track down the road to socialism is because the liberals who dominate the mass media are at the wheel.

In times past, the media often served as the watchdog of government; now it serves as the makers of government and government policy. Just as tyrannical governments of the past once banned freedom of the press, now the all-powerful media giants ban the other side of the story. There's no difference.

They ban the opposition by burying their side of a story deep inside the newspaper, or, more often, by not printing it at all. The ban is as effective as any tyrant's edict to ban all opposition. The mass media has become our modern day-tyrant; it is the worst oppressor of freedom of speech this country has ever had.

So what's the solution? Quite simple, really. Freedom-loving people who want to hear both sides of the story have got to get into the media business. Not just as news reporters, but as owners of newspapers, magazines, and radio and TV stations. If we are to stop this country's deterioration into a socialist state, getting the "other side of the story" back into the mass media is a must.

Terrorism and war

Which wars work best? The ones we fight or the ones we avoid?

(originally published in November 2006)

History is supposed to teach us the lessons of wars past so we won't blunder into stupid wars in the present. Since I have mixed feelings about our War on Terrorism and our war in Iraq, I thought I'd review the wars America has fought in my lifetime, as well as the ones we avoided. Maybe it will paint a path for America to follow now.

I was born one year before the end of World War II, which history calls "the good war" because it saved Europe and possibly the world from the tyranny of the Nazis. We lost 400,000 dead, the world lost 60 million dead, European and Japanese civilizations were nearly destroyed, and Soviet Communism, a system at least as murderous as the Nazis, emerged from the war a superpower. But we forced American-style democracy on Germany and Japan, and after they got over the bitterness of defeat, they prospered under democracy and became allies of America. America was the only real victor in that war. Our homeland had not been devastated by bombs, and we emerged as the most powerful nation in the world.

The Korean Conflict raged while I was a boy. That war ended in stalemate after 50,000 Americans died, but our side, South Korea, went on to prosper under American-style democracy while the other side, North Korea, undergoes famines and starvation to this day under a regime that sells arms to the highest bidder and is working to develop a nuclear bomb that the buyer will no doubt aim at America. We still have to maintain an army in South Korea.

Then came Vietnam. My college friends were among the 50,000 Americans killed there, but after public pressure from back home, America abruptly left and ushered in a blood-letting in Southeast Asia that killed millions of civilians in Vietnam and Cambodia. Vietnam is the war we seldom talk about today because it accomplished nothing but the destruction of the cream of America's youth. Today, as before the war, Vietnam does not openly threaten America.

Most recently, we've had America's two wars against Iraq, both spectacularly successful militarily. We had to fight the first war because Iraq invaded Kuwait and threatened our oil supply, a fuel we probably should have made ourselves independent of a long time ago. We fought the second one because we thought Iraq was trying to develop a nuclear bomb that could possibly be sold to terrorists. This last contention is vehemently debated now by politicians running for office. But we are in Iraq nevertheless, with more than 2,000 Americans dead and no end in sight.

Along with Iraq, we have our ongoing War on Terrorism, launched when radical Islamists brought down the twin towers in New York. We killed or captured much of Al Qaeda, main sponsor of the radical Islamists, after invading Afghanistan. Now the War on Terrorism and the war in Iraq have sort of combined, with a civil war among Shia and Sunni Arabs thrown in, and with Syria and Iran and others fanning the flames. It's become a big mess.

Here's the wars we didn't fight in my lifetime:

We never fought the Soviet Union, the most dangerous enemy of America in my lifetime. We would have won because we had better technology than them, but many of our cities would have fallen to nuclear bombs. As capitalists, we understood that Communism was an unsound economic system, so we wisely pursued a policy of "mutually assured destruction," keeping the Soviets at bay until the inevitable happened. It was the wisest war we never fought. The Soviet Union is now a bunch of separate countries, sort of third-worldish, and no longer a threat to us.

We also never fought the Red Chinese. This Communist system was never strong enough to pose as serious a threat as the Soviets, and as the Soviets stumbled under their own bad economic policy, the Chinese cracked its doors open to the West to see if it could avoid the same fate. Luckily, that much-maligned former president, Richard Nixon, seized the opportunity and extended America's hand. China is now the workshop of the world, prosperous, and less and less Communist every day. It is simply evolving out of its tyrannical former self and into a prosperous capitalist society. The fact that it remains Communist and godless does not seem too relevant anymore. This is the second wisest war we never fought.

So in light of all these past wars and avoided wars, what can be deduced to guide us today?

Obviously, the wars we avoided worked out best. No one got killed, civilizations were not devastated, and America was triumphant. That was because American-style capitalism was allowed to do its thing. Our system is simply better than anyone else's. The Soviet Union learned that too late, but China learned it just in time.

All the real wars had disappointing results. Even World War II, which I don't think America could have avoided, ended up empowering the Communists for half a century.

Our current wars don't look promising in light of history. Sure, we can defeat any enemy in the short-term, but history says that for success in the long-term we need to convert the enemy to American-style capitalism so they, too, can prosper. I don't know how we are going to do that. I don't think anyone does. But just as it did with Communism, I think it will make Islamic jihadism a moot point.

Something unsaid about
Timothy McVeigh's execution

(originally published in July 2001)

There's something unsaid about the Timothy McVeigh execution. Many of us can feel it but are afraid to express it for fear of being labeled a Timothy McVeigh sympathizer, or for fear of being charged with condoning the murder of 168 innocent people, including 19 children, even for fear of being targeted by our government as terrorists ourselves.

What is unsaid can be inferred from the absence of internet e-mail or newspaper snail mail condemning McVeigh. In fact, it is the absence of much discussion at all about him. Sure, mass media reporters talk about him, and our government does, but ordinary people don't.

When our federal government caused the deaths of 76 people at Waco, Texas, April 19, 1993, exactly two years before McVeigh struck, the internet and local newspapers were aflood with heated chatter about how horrible and unjust our government was. And when the government acquitted its agents of all wrongdoing and convicted the surviving Branch Davidians of minor offenses, but sentenced them to 30 and 40-year prison terms anyway, there was outrage once more. You could not download your e-mail, surf the web, or read your local newspaper without being inundated with the outrage.

But for McVeigh's death on closed-circuit TV in the first federal execution in 38 years, there is relative silence from ordinary people, both on the internet and in the local newspaper. Very little e-mail or letters to the editor, very little discussion pro or con. Why is that? We can't quite put our finger on it, can we, or we dare not express the horror in our heart at the moment, and the implications for freedom in this country.

Let's review what many of us feel:

• We accept the fact that Timothy McVeigh is a murderer and we sympathize with the victims' families. But we also understand that our government's agents killed 76 people at Waco, including 19 children, many of whom died agonizing deaths vomiting their stomachs out from the CS gas grenades lobbed into the building. We sympathize with those victims' families, also.

• We accept the fact that Timothy McVeigh should pay with his life, but we cannot accept the fact that our government's agents got off scott-free for Waco, and some were even promoted in its aftermath.

• We cannot accept the fact that the mainstream media remembers the victims of Oklahoma City, but is silent about the victims of Waco. You'd think no one died at Waco, or that there were no dead children there, or that there is no connection between the two events.

• We are outraged by the fact that McVeigh showed no remorse for the deaths of the 19 children at the Murrah Building, but we are also outraged that our government showed no remorse for the deaths of the 19 children at Waco.

• And no, we do not buy the government and mass media line that the Waco victims chose their end by their lack of cooperation with the FBI agents, BATF agents, and the tanks that besieged

184

their home. They were nutty members of a religious cult? So what! Since when is that a crime?

Our government created McVeigh by its actions at Waco, just as it creates terrorists around the world by its "police" actions in various parts of the globe. Is it any wonder that one of these created terrorists, one among the millions of people who were outraged by Waco, felt unable to gain justice through the normal legal channels, and sought revenge by trying to get at the BATF agents housed on an upper floor of the Murrah Building?

Blowing up the Murrah Building was a horrible act by McVeigh, for sure, but that is what terrorists do. Look around the world at what the Arabs have done in Israel, or what they did here in the U.S., in New York, in 1993, at the World Trade Center. We view them as criminals, but they view themselves as justice-seekers.

Terrorism is a terrible thing, whether it's committed deliberately by a government against its citizens or by an individual who strikes out in a misguided revengeful rage.

When the anniversary of Waco and the Murrah Building arrived April 19, I mourned all the victims, both those of our government and those of Timothy McVeigh. And with McVeigh's execution, I am saddened that his is to be the only justice delivered.

McVeigh's execution is a major turning point for America. We now all see the double standard in action, in all its horrific nakedness: The lone terrorist dies, while the government terrorists go free. We may be rid of McVeigh, but we will understand that far more powerful terrorists still lurk among us.

Postscript: This Timothy McVeigh article was very popular, reprinted in many media, and I was invited to be a guest on several radio shows. But its publication preceded by only two months the terrorist attack that brought down New York's twin-trade towers, and the climate for any type of anti-Government sentiment, or perceived sympathy towards terrorists, changed instantly and dramatically. This would be a dangerous column to publish today, likely subjecting me to interrogation by the FBI and probably causing economic harassment and hardship for my company, Backwoods Home Magazine.

To me, America's current War on Terrorism smacks of the unending war in George Orwell's futuristic novel, 1984. Government now has the excuse it needs to stifle dissent against how it operates, whether abroad or at home. If you speak out against the imprisonment by our Government of "enemy combatants" without any charges being filed against them, you are branded as anti-American. Ditto if you protest the Government's many new laws that invade Americans' privacy or curtail their freedoms. This War on Terrorism could go on forever. It is tailor-made for a Government to run rough-shod over its own people, while pretending to protect them against a foreign enemy.

Am I just being paranoid? I hope so!

How do you keep yourself safe?

(originally published in November 2001)

The overwhelming concerns for most Americans in the wake of the terrorist attacks at New York's World Trade Center come down to this: How do I keep myself and my family safe? That's as it should be because if you keep yourself safe, you help keep us all safe, and you help keep the nation safe.

If you are a regular reader of this magazine, you probably already do the things that keep you safe: You own a gun and are practiced in using it, you have about a two-year supply of food that is rotated so it is fresh and nutritious, and you have implemented one of many schemes to keep your home sufficiently warm, well-lit, and otherwise prepared for any emergency.

If you are not a regular reader of this magazine, you may be experiencing a lot of anxiety right now because that is what the New York terrorists attacks were designed, in part, to do—to scare the American people. And if you live in a big city, you are probably particularly anxious because you know that cities make better terrorist targets than small country towns and homesteads, and you probably have all sorts of laws against owning or carrying guns, and you are not inclined to keep a supply of food or fuel, and you aren't prepared for anything. I'm not really sure what you can do.

Travelling is a different matter. Even the well-prepared readers of this magazine sometimes travel, even on airlines. What can you do when you travel?

Ever since the terrorists attacks, I have been repeatedly told by the politicians and talking heads on all the television news channels that this is not a time for "finger pointing," so I guess I shouldn't point out the fact that our liberal politicians have made it virtually impossible for us to protect ourselves when we travel. Even if you own a gun, you cannot legally take it anywhere except maybe in your home state. It's good to hear some people on TV at least talking about putting armed sky marshals back on planes, arming the pilots, and making the barrier between cockpit and cabin impenetrable.

But they'll never let you carry your own gun with you when you travel, no matter how many hours of training you go through. Back when they had armed sky marshals aboard planes, a lot of passengers complained that it made them nervous, so as soon as the funding ran out they discontinued the practice. Imagine the difference a gun could have made in these terrorist attacks?

So what can you do? Well, you can determine ahead of time that you will never ever consent to becoming a sheep in a hostage situation. Let's take a lesson from those brave people aboard United Flight 93, which crashed in Pennsylvania, short of its terrorist target. Some of the passengers had learned via cell phone that the terrorists were crashing the hijacked planes into buildings, so they decided to try to stop them. They apparently succeeded by rushing the terrorists.

You can prepare yourself for a similar situation by becoming an island of resolve ahead of time. Simply decide you will never go down without a fight and prepare yourself accordingly, whether that means taking a martial arts course or making some other contingency plan. Hit the terrorists with your laptop computer, or with your fists if that is the only weapon you have. But determine now that you will never be a passive victim.

What help can you expect from politicians and bureaucrats in the wake of these terrorist attacks? At Boston's Logan Airport, they banned the sale of knives because the terrorists apparently used box cutters and plastic knives as their weapons. If the terrorists had used guns, I can guarantee you the response would have been more gun control. (What we actually need is a national concealed-carry law.)

The politicians and TV talking heads talk mainly about a war against terrorists that will make them stop their terrorism. Maybe that will work. We could bomb countries like Afghanistan back into the Stone Age, but they already live a near Stone Age existence after having undergone some 20-odd years of nearly continuous war. We could assassinate people like Osama bin Laden and Saddam Hussein, but that still leaves millions of people around the world who hate Americans due to our "policeman of the world" foreign policy. But now I'm engaging in finger pointing, and the politicians have told me I shouldn't do that.

So my advice comes down to this: Take care of yourself and your family. If you think you can handle it, buy a gun, learn how to use it, get a concealed-carry permit, and keep it with you so you can protect yourself against terrorists and criminals alike.

Then, grab the nearest gun-grabbing liberal you can find and throw him out a window.

Smallpox —
it's worth worrying about

(originally published in March 2003)

Is a smallpox epidemic brought about by terrorists something to worry about? After all, it is a horrible disease, killing 30% of its victims and terribly disfiguring, sometimes blinding, those who survive.

We've all read or heard something about smallpox, how Bush has ordered the vaccinating of the military and a half million medical "first responders," and how he's ordered more smallpox vaccine be ready for the general public by early 2004. Does he know something we don't?

And there's been a lot of discussion on how terrorists might attack us with smallpox: Infected jihad volunteers walking among us, aerosolized containers containing weaponized smallpox placed surreptitiously on the walls of shopping malls and airports.

Most media pundits have concluded that it's a very small threat. Jihad volunteers would be too sick, and too noticeably ill, if they had smallpox to be able to walk around infecting people, and getting hold of weaponized smallpox would be about as hard to do as winning the lottery.

But I am a media pundit who has spent the last two months reading everything I can about smallpox, and I am very worried

190

that a smallpox attack is the threat we should all take seriously. For one, I think getting hold of weaponized smallpox will be a lot easier than most people think; after all, someone got hold of weaponized anthrax and sent it though the mail shortly after 9-11.

But I also have another reason, a fact that has been overlooked in the media, it being perhaps too deeply embedded in the literature detailing the 12,000-year history of this greatest of all human plagues: A person previously vaccinated with the smallpox vaccine, then exposed to smallpox, can get a mild case of smallpox if his vaccination is so old it doesn't give him full protection. He may not even know he's sick, he will be able to walk around fine, he will have few symptoms, perhaps a light rash, but he will then be capable of passing on full-blown smallpox to someone else, especially to our children who, almost without exception, have never been vaccinated.

This disturbing fact is one of the reasons why the "ring method" of controlling smallpox outbreaks was used back in the 1960s and '70s to finally eradicate the disease. With the ring method, all contacts of a smallpox victim were closely watched, vaccinated, and forcibly isolated if necessary until it was certain they had not contracted smallpox, even a mild form. Then, a second ring of people who had had contacts with the first ring was established to make sure they hadn't been infected.

They took no chances. They knew that smallpox was persistent. It could remain alive in the clothing and bedding of infected patients, even lay dried but alive in the dust of a patient's room, for months after the patient had either died or recovered. That's why disinfecting a smallpox patient's room was critical. Smallpox had already killed 300-500 million people in the 20th century, which is three to five times the number of people killed in all that century's wars combined. The final defeat of smallpox, the only disease to ever have been eradicated, is an achievement at least as significant as landing a man on the moon.

But if enough jihad volunteers with waning smallpox vaccinations (and that includes half the human race since most vaccinations stopped in the '70s) were to expose themselves to smallpox so that a few of them got a mild but contagious case of smallpox, they could then walk among us and bring smallpox back again to plague humanity. And here in the U.S., we wouldn't even know we had been attacked until two weeks later when our symptoms started showing up. By that time, the jihad attackers could have travelled to dozens of cities in America and infected hundreds. The "ring method" of controlling the disease would not work because the jihad volunteers would not cooperate. They would be like so many Typhoid Marys. And the attackers wouldn't even have to commit suicide; they would recover and escape. We wouldn't even know how we had been attacked.

It is an impossible attack strategy to defend against, except if we resort to mass smallpox vaccinations. But that may be a very difficult strategy to sustain in light of the fact that data from the 1960s and '70s smallpox eradication program indicates that the vaccinia vaccine itself, which is made from cowpox, will kill one or two Americans per million vaccinated and gravely sicken at least another 2,000. And that data does not take into account our modern day situation: Millions of Americans with eczema-related skin conditions, AIDS, and other immune system problems who absolutely should not be given the vaccine unless they are in imminent danger of contracting smallpox.

Even an attack of this type that produced only a handful of smallpox cases would virtually shut down our society.

That's a big problem on a grand scale I hope the nation never has to face. But it is definitely worth worrying about.

At the individual level, it's less of a problem. If you're not among those in the "at-risk" group, you can get vaccinated when the vaccine is made available to the public early next year—or earlier if there is an actual attack. The vaccine will protect you for up to four days after exposure to smallpox. If you're in the "at risk" group (I am because I've got an eczema-related skin condition) and we do get attacked, you can formulate a plan now, as I have, to isolate yourself and family (I'll also vaccinate my kids) with lots of food and survival stuff until the threat passes.

What are the odds of such an attack? What were the odds of them flying planes loaded with people into the WTC and Pentagon?

Dark Winter
**a simulated terrorist attack on three American cities
using weaponized smallpox**

(originally published in May 2003)

Historically, smallpox has been the most deadly of all diseases for humans, killing between 300 and 500 million in the last century alone, far more than the 111 million people killed in all that century's wars combined. It is easily spread, kills 30% of those infected, and terribly scars and sometimes blinds those who survive. It was declared eradicated from Earth in 1980, but the Soviet Union has acknowledged maintaining a secret biological weapons program since then that employed 60,000 technicians and scientists. One fear is that some of the smallpox the Soviets worked with has gotten into terrorist hands, or that unemployed Soviet scientists desperate for money have been hired by Iraq, Al Qaida, or other terrorists.

June 22-23, 2001, nearly three months before the attack that toppled New York's World Trade towers, the United States conducted a major simulation of a terrorist smallpox attack against three American cities. It was named Dark Winter, and it lived up to its name. Within seven weeks, one million Americans were dead, and the disease had spread to 25 states and 13 foreign countries. In the face of the out-of-control epidemic, panic had spread across America, interrupting vital services such as food deliveries to supermarkets, and our government considered the possibility of a nuclear response, although against whom it was not clear.

Following is a reenactment of that exercise, edited for brevity but containing all the essential elements. The exercise took place at Andrews Air Force Base in Maryland and was attended by many senior level government officials. Participating institutions included the Johns Hopkins Center for Civilian Biodefense Strategies, the Center for Strategic and International Studies, the Oklahoma National Memorial Institute for the Prevention of Terrorism, and the Analytic Services Institute for Homeland Security.

Former U.S. Senator Sam Nunn of Georgia played the President of the United States, Governor Frank Keating of Oklahoma played himself, five senior journalists who worked for major news organizations participated in mock news briefings, and a number of other participants played various key government positions ranging from the Director of Central Intelligence to key government health advisors. Fifty people connected with U.S. bioterrorism policy preparedness observed the exercise.

The goal of the exercise was to increase awareness among government officials of the danger of such an attack and to examine the decision challenges the highest levels of government would face if confronted with a biological attack. The ultimate aim was to improve strategies of response.

Smallpox was chosen as the disease because historically it has been the most feared and deadly of diseases and one of the more likely choices for terrorists. It is not only easily spread from one person to another, but there is no effective medical treatment. It may also be unstoppable in an unvaccinated population, and since the United States' mandatory vaccination program was stopped in

1972, the U.S. population is very susceptible to smallpox. Even that part of the population that was vaccinated as late as 1972 may have little or no protection against the disease.

Although smallpox was declared eradicated in 1980, two official repositories of the variola virus were kept: One at the Centers for Disease Control and Prevention in Atlanta, and the other at the Russian State Research Center for Virology and Biotechnology in Koltsovo, Novosibirsk in central Siberia. Those supplies were to be used for scientific research and vaccine development, but it is now known that both countries maintained secret biological weapons programs since 1980. By 1990, the Soviet Union had a facility capable of producing 80 to 100 tons of smallpox a year, and it typically warehoused 20 tons. Although Russia and the United States have since abandoned their biological weapons programs, other countries still have them. It is thought that several rogue states like North Korea and Iraq and possibly terrorists have obtained samples of the smallpox virus.

Although the exercise took only two days, it simulated a time span of two weeks occurring between December 9-22, 2002. The exercise involved three National Security Council (NSC) meetings taking place on December 9, 15, and 22, with the participants being made aware of evolving details of the attack and being required to establish strategies and make policy decisions to deal with it.

Exercise controllers acted as special assistants and deputies, providing facts and suggesting policy options to deal with the smallpox outbreak. Simulated newspaper coverage and TV video clips of the ensuing epidemic were also shown to participants, and various simulated memoranda, intelligence updates, and top-level assessments of the spread of the epidemic were provided to key players whose jobs would normally require such information.

Each of the three NSC meetings began with controllers giving the NSC players briefings on the progress of the attack, an assessment of who the perpetrators might be, the response of the public, the comments of foreign governments, and any other information they would normally receive in such an emergency.

Several assumptions were made for this exercise, based on historical evidence and a variety of data related to susceptibility to smallpox:

• **Assumption 1:** It was assumed that the initial attack was from "weaponized smallpox," similar to what the former Soviet Union would have developed in its secret bioweapons program.

This would be a far more efficient way of attacking the U.S. than with, say, infected jihad volunteers walking among the U.S. population. Weaponized smallpox can be aerosolized and dispersed in a variety of ways, such as attaching an aerosol device filled with weaponized smallpox, complete with a timer, to the wall of a shopping mall, airport, or ventilation system of an enclosed stadium, or attaching a spraying device to an unmanned drone (UAV) that has been programmed with global positioning (GPS) maps and flying it over a populated area.

• **Assumption 2:** The U.S. population's "herd immunity" to smallpox was 20%, so that 228 million of its citizens were highly susceptible to infection.

This is a matter of debate. It is known that 42% of the population has never received a smallpox vaccination, and the remainder have declining immunity from vaccinations about 30 years ago. No one knows for sure, but epidemiologic data suggest that initial vaccination gives protection for 5 to 10 years, while revaccination gives even greater protection, possibly more than 10 years. Those who have been vaccinated twice, then, say as a child and while in the military, should have the greatest immunity.

• **Assumption 3:** The transmission rate of the disease was 10:1; that is, each infected person infected 10 others.

Although transmission rates have varied widely historically depending on susceptibility of a population, the strain of disease, and various social, demographic, political, and economic factors, the simulation designers considered a 10:1 transmission rate a conservative estimate. The U.S. population, they pointed out, is highly susceptible because vaccinations stopped in this country 30 years ago. Also, we are a highly mobile society. By the time the first victims are diagnosed with smallpox (9-17 day incuba-tion period), the disease will have already begun spreading to a second generation of victims. Some of the initial victims and the second generation of victims will have travelled to other cities by that time. Since few American doctors have ever seen a case of smallpox, and since the initial symptoms resemble flu, diagnosis is liable to be slow.

For this simulation, the 10:1 estimate was based on 34 smallpox outbreaks in the past involving cases of smallpox being acciden-tally imported into a country that no longer had endemic small-pox. Twenty four of the outbreaks occurred in winter, which is the time when smallpox spreads most readily and which is the time within which the simulated attack occurs. Of these 24, 6 out-breaks most closed paralleled the conditions of the Dark Winter exercise, and they were used to make the 10:1 estimate. The num-ber of second generation cases in those 6 outbreaks ranged from 10 to 19.

One reason the 10:1 estimate is thought to be on the conservative side is because of the 1972 outbreak in Yugoslavia, which encompassed many of the aspects one finds today in American society, namely, a great number of susceptible people and a wide geographic dispersion of cases. In that outbreak, a man on a religious pilgrimage to Mecca and Medina was infected with smallpox while in Iraq, then brought it back to Yugoslavia. His infection was not diagnosed, nor were the 11 people he infected suspected of having smallpox. Not until 140 new cases developed was the epidemic recognized as smallpox. Some 35 people died from this single initial infection.

• **Assumption 4:** The U.S. Centers for Disease Control and Prevention (CDC) had 12 million doses of vaccine available at the time of the exercise.

The CDC actually had 15.4 million doses, but practical experience from the 1960s and '70s smallpox eradication programs showed that it was common to lose 20% of a vial's vaccine due to inefficiencies and waste.

• **Assumption 5:** In the initial attack at three shopping malls in Oklahoma City, Philadelphia, and Atlanta, 3,000 people were infected.

This is considered a plausible scenario scientifically since it would take only 30 grams of weaponized smallpox to infect 3,000 people via an aerosol attack.

The 1st NSC meeting, December 9, 2002
The initial attack:

On December 9, 2002, during the first of three NSC meetings that will take place in this simulation, the 12 NSC members are told that a smallpox outbreak has occurred in the U.S. In Oklahoma, 12 cases of smallpox have been confirmed, with 14 more suspected. There are also suspected cases of smallpox in Georgia and Pennsylvania.

The governor of Oklahoma, Frank Keating, who is in town to make a speech, attends the meeting. NSC members are briefed on the disease, its lethality, its contagion, and the availability of smallpox vaccine.

All this takes place against a backdrop of the following geopolitical situation:

• Iraq is again threatening to invade Kuwait, and leaders of Kuwait, the United Arab Emirates, and Bahrain have requested the U.S., Britain, and France deploy troops to the region. The NSC meeting has been called to consider deploying forces.

• Since sanctions against Iraq had been lifted six months prior, it has been discovered that Saddam Hussein is aggressively pursuing a bioweapons program.

• Several top scientists from the former Soviet secret bioweapons program are believed to have been working in Iraq and Iran for the past year.

• An Al Qaida terrorist was recently caught trying to buy plutonium and biological pathogens from Russia.

President Nunn informs the NSC members that the agenda of the meeting has changed, that the U.S. has been subjected to a suspected smallpox attack, and that it could be related to their anticipated decision to deploy troops to the Mideast. No one has yet taken credit for the attack.

He introduces Governor Keating, who says hospital emergency rooms in Oklahoma City hospitals are very crowded and that many in the hospital staff have failed to show up for work, fearing a smallpox infection they might bring home to their families. The media is broadcasting nonstop news about the smallpox outbreak, and the Governor is already considering calling out the National Guard if fear continues to grow among the populace. He has already declared a state of emergency and requests the President do the same. He goes before the news cameras in a few hours, he says, and he'd like to be able to tell the people of Oklahoma that all 3.5 million of them will get the smallpox vaccine within 72 hours.

The NSC is then briefed on smallpox, using various slides of actual smallpox cases and statistics relating to the progression, spread, and lethality of the disease: U.S. doctors have no experience with smallpox, and there is no rapid diagnosis or treatment. Isolation or vaccination are the only defenses. Only 12 million doses of vaccine are available, and a CDC contract for an additional 40 million doses will not be filled until 2004. The worldwide supply of vaccine is 60 million doses, but some of it is believed worthless due to inadequate storage by some countries.

The NSC members are told that the CDC has sent 100,000 doses of smallpox vaccine to Oklahoma, with vaccinations restricted to infected people, their close contacts, and investigators.

Council members are also told that the attack most likely occurred about December 1, due to at least a 7-day incubation period for the disease. The second generation of cases, then, would be about December 20, 11 days away. Urgent action is needed to halt the spread of the disease, but a modern, urban, mobile population, coupled with a limited supply of vaccine, does not offer encouraging prospects for controlling the outbreak.

The FBI tells the Council they will have 200 agents vaccinated and sent to Oklahoma within 24 hours, but they have no leads as yet. Several possible culprits are named: Iraq, Iran, North Korea,

China, Russia all have the capability. But anyone who has obtained samples of smallpox, possibly from an unemployed Soviet scientist, could grow smallpox and launch an attack.

Council members consider their options. The CDC and local authorities would already be isolating victims and their closest contacts. Should public gatherings be curtailed and schools closed? How should the available vaccine be distributed? Should the National Guard be activated, and should it be under state or federal control? Should there be mandatory or voluntary vaccinations? What should the public be told? What should be done about the deployment of troops to the Mideast?

They agree to inform the public quickly and completely to ensure cooperation with disease control measures. They decide to use the "ring method" of vaccination, which worked so successfully in eradicating the disease in the 1960s and '70s. With the ring method, all first contacts with the victim are vaccinated, then a second ring of secondary contacts are vaccinated. The NSC decides the ring method should also be used in other states, should the virus break out there. For strategic purposes, they reserve 1 million doses of vaccine for Department of Defense (DOD) needs, and instruct the DOD to determine its priorities. They also decide to deploy an additional aircraft carrier battle group to the Persian Gulf to join the one already there.

The final action of the NSC is to prepare a presidential statement for the news media, which the President delivers to a nationwide audience from the press room.

The 2nd NSC meeting, December 15, 2002
The outbreak spreads:
The second NSC meeting opens with a review of the following news video clips:

202

• 300 people are dead and 2,000 are infected in 15 states. Hospitals are overwhelmed as tens of thousand of sick or fearful people seek medical help. Many hospital employees are not showing up for work.

• The epidemic has spread to Canada, Mexico, and the United Kingdom, with Canada and Mexico asking the U.S. for vaccine.

• Violence has broken out in some areas, with riots around a vaccination site in Philadelphia leaving two dead. Police and the National Guard are trying to control the crowds.

• Many countries have closed their borders to people travelling from the U.S. unless they can show proof of recent smallpox vaccination.

• Governor Keating is considering closing all stores to try and halt the spread of the disease. Malls across the country are already virtually deserted. The Governor has closed all schools and universities and cancelled all sporting events.

• The federal government is being widely criticized from all quarters for failure to have an adequate smallpox vaccine on hand. The lone pharmaceutical company capable of making smallpox vaccine says that at most it can produce 4 million doses per month, even if all FDA regulations are waived. Russia has offered to provide 4 million doses of vaccine.

• Panic buying is beginning to occur in some cities as food deliveries are slowed by the reluctance of truckers to go into areas with smallpox. There are sporadic reports of people of Arab appearance being assaulted on the street.

A memo is given to the Attorney General. It clarifies the Stafford Act, the Posse Comitatus Act, the Federal Quarantine Law, the Insurrection Act, and Martial Law, all laws designed to invoke federal authority in a national emergency. Among other things, the laws would allow the President to declare a national emergency and use military troops to quell civil disturbances, authorize the forced inoculation and isolation of people who could spread a communicable disease, restrict travel, dispose of bodies in ways contrary to personal beliefs, suspend habeas corpus (that is, arrest without due process), and curtail other liberties as needed.

Another memo to the FBI Director and Attorney General states there is a high probability that the attack came from another state or a state-sponsored terrorist group, and that an initial analysis of the smallpox used indicates it came from Soviet Union stocks or North Korea. The memo notes that as little as two years ago North Korean Special Forces were still receiving smallpox vaccine.

The President is handed a memo suggesting it may be problematic going forward with a war in the Persian Gulf, given the severity of the domestic crisis. He addresses the council members, announcing that the Secretary of State is ill and hospitalized. He says the lack of vaccine and the tactics of some states to stop the epidemic has led to serious economic disruption and civil unrest in some areas.

The Chair of the Deputies Committee, Dr. Tara O'Toole, outlines the progress of the epidemic and says all cases appear related to three initial attacks in Oklahoma, Georgia, and Pennsylvania. Vaccine, unfortunately, is running out amid growing political pressure to vaccinate more broadly. One million doses of vaccine are still being held for military personnel facing the potential war in the Persian Gulf. With all the vaccine that has been distributed, 1.25 million doses remain.

Dr. O'Toole further states that there is growing public demand for the forcible relocation of infected people to isolated facilities. She says contacts of infected people are not complying sufficiently with voluntary home isolation. There is also dangerous misinformation in some media about good vaccine and bad vaccine, advice to flee cities, claims that poor neighborhoods are being denied vaccine, and hate speech directed at certain ethnic groups.

The FEMA Director delivers his remarks: Health care facilities have become nonfunctional in some communities due to overcrowding and workers staying away from their jobs. At least 20 hospitals have closed their doors in Oklahoma. In many states, National Guard troops are providing security at hospitals, even delivering food and critical supplies. Many states have prohibited public gatherings, stopped transportation, and closed airports.

Once again, the NSC considers its options. Members decide to leave the National Guard, as well as quarantine and isolation issues, in the hands of the states. They will accept the vaccine from Russia and proceed with a crash program to manufacture vaccine even though liability issues have not been resolved. They opt for mandatory isolation of all smallpox victims in dedicated facilities. They will encourage voluntary isolation of contacts using National Guard and Defense Department resources to supply food. Federal travel restrictions will be established, and penalties will be imposed for the promulgation of dangerous information.

An intelligence memo is given to NSC members: It indicates that a new exclusionary zone has been established by Iraq around a suspected bioresearch facility near Samarra. Activity at the facility appears normal, but villages for a 10-mile radius around it appear to have been abandoned.

In a memo delivered to the Attorney General, there are reports of increasing incidents of violence, mainly against people with dark skin or who appear Arab-American. Two mosques have been defaced and one burned in the last 24 hours. In downtown Chicago, three dark-skinned youths were shot dead, apparently because they looked Middle Eastern. The ACLU has sued Pennsylvania over the issues of mandatory vaccination and curtailment of transportation.

The NSC watches a newsclip in which the Governor of Texas announces the suspension of all travel between Texas and Oklahoma. He urges other governors to do the same, and he strongly criticizes the federal government for being "unable or unwilling to prevent the spread of the smallpox virus."

President Nunn addresses the nation on national TV. He relates the gravity of the crisis and appeals for Americans to remain calm and work together to defeat the virus and to heed the advice of their elected leaders and health officials.

The 3rd NSC meeting, December 22, 2002
A crisis out of control:

The third and final NSC meeting opens with a review of news video clips:

• The number of smallpox cases has reached 16,000, with 1,000 people now dead. The epidemic has spread to 25 states and 10 other countries. Although investigation suggests all cases are related to the initial attack in three states, the evidence does not rule out additional or ongoing attacks.

• The U.S. is suffering severe economic damage. In Atlanta and Philadelphia, most businesses are closed and massive traffic jams are occurring across the state as people try to flee the disease.

• A *New York Times* poll indicates that most Americans think that the state and federal governments have lost control of the epidemic. A CNN/Gallup poll says nearly half of Americans think the President should use nuclear weapons against any nation proven responsible for the smallpox attack.

• Violence is spreading across the nation as individuals try to keep others suspected of having smallpox at a distance. In New York, two police officers and three family members were killed when the police tried to escort two family members with smallpox to an isolation area.

Then, Dr. O'Toole once again outlines the progress of the epidemic for the NSC:

• In the past 48 hours there have been 14,000 new cases. Of the 1,000 dead, 200 have been from reactions to vaccination. It is estimated that 5,000 more will die within the next two weeks.

• The vaccine has now been depleted, and the U.S. can produce only 12 million unlicensed doses a month, beginning in four weeks.

• A major impact on the U.S. economy continues and there are shortages of many types of food across the nation. People are fleeing cities after the announcement of new smallpox cases.

The NSC asks for a worst-case scenario. It is stark:

• By the end of the second generation of smallpox cases (about January 3), 30,000 will be infected and 10,000 dead.

• By the end of Generation 3 (January 20), 300,000 will be infected and 100,000 dead.

• By the end of Generation 4 (February 6, which is 7 weeks after the start of the epidemic), 3 million will be infected and 1 million dead.

A memo is given to the Secretary of State:

• Russia, France, and Nigeria are demanding the U.S. share any vaccine it has to help fight the overseas spread of the epidemic.

• Cuba has offered to sell smallpox vaccine to the U.S. Cuba claims it has the know-how to produce the vaccine quickly.

Another memo is handed to the Director of the FBI and the Director of Central Intelligence (DCI):

• A credible Iraqi defector claims Iraq is behind the smallpox attack. Iraq has previously denied involvement, but has also warned the U.S. that it will retaliate against any U.S. attack in "highly damaging ways."

Finally, a printed message is handed to all members of the NSC. It states that the *New York Times, Washington Post*, and *USA Today* have received anonymous letters demanding the U.S. withdraw its forces from the Persian Gulf and Saudi Arabia. The letter claims responsibility for the smallpox attack and contains a generic fingerprint of the smallpox strain matching the fingerprint of the strain causing the current epidemic. Unless the U.S. forces withdraw in one week, it warns of renewed attacks using smallpox, anthrax, and plague.

The Dark Winter exercise ends with the NSC discussing how to respond. If the American people demand they use nuclear weapons, against who? Should they withdraw U.S. troops from the Persian Gulf? And finally, with no vaccine remaining and the epidemic out of control, how do they control the current spread of smallpox and any new attacks with disease?

End of Dark Winter exercise

Astonishing! The United States had been brought to its knees by a virus delivered covertly by terrorists who lurk in the dark recesses of the world. Few thought it remotely possible before the exercise, but afterwards many inside and outside of Government became alarmed at the possibility.

The Dark Winter exercise was no trivial undertaking. It was carefully planned and orchestrated, primarily by the prestigious Johns Hopkins University in Baltimore, Maryland, to answer one question: Could America withstand an attack of human-inflicted disease. The answer was a resounding No!—at least in the case of smallpox. We flunked the exercise on a catastrophic scale.

Three months after the exercise, the U.S. was subjected to the September 11 attacks against the World Trade Center in New York City and the subsequent anthrax mail attacks in Washington, D.C. Suddenly the attacks of terrorists were not just the stuff of "what-if" simulations like Dark Winter. Our Government began working on defense strategies against such attacks, and it started evaluating its stocks of smallpox vaccine.

The vaccine situation is different today than it was in June of 2001 when the Dark Winter exercise took place. The U.S. has found more vaccine than we thought we had, and we have diluted other vaccine to make it stretch far enough to cover the American population. There are still questions about the effectiveness of this diluted vaccine after so many years in storage, but new vaccine to cover the entire population is being manufactured and will be ready in early 2004. Risks associated with the vaccine are another serious consideration not discussed in the Dark Winter simulation. I discuss risks in the associated article, "How safe is smallpox vaccine?"

How safe is smallpox vaccine?

(originally published in May 2003)

At the start of 2003, the United States began the vaccination against smallpox of half a million health care workers so America can respond to a possible terrorist smallpox attack. It is only the beginning of a plan to vaccinate millions of Americans, beginning with health care workers and the military. The fear is that terrorists, and possibly Iraq, have acquired the deadly and disfiguring smallpox virus and intend to use it against us.

Many people may think no sane human being would consider using a disease like smallpox as a weapon. After all, even the diabolical Nazis of World War II possessed nerve agents and biological weapons but refrained from using them, even as they were bombed into obliteration during the last months of the war. But, think again. According to many Muslim terrorists, it is God's will that America the Infidel be destroyed.

It is not an unheard-of rationale. In at least one documented case during the conquest of the Americas, a British colonel deliberately distributed smallpox-infected blankets to Indians, which led to an epidemic among them. And during the Spanish conquest of the Aztecs, which coincided with another smallpox epidemic among the Indians, a Spanish priest wrote in his diary: "Thank you heavenly Father for sending this plague to destroy our enemies." There is even some evidence that the British tried to spread smallpox among the Colonists, and during America's own Civil War, there is an undocumented report of a Confederate supplying unsuspecting Union soldiers with smallpox-infected blankets.

Man, historically, has always justified his most reprehensible actions, and Muslim crusaders will have no problem justifying a smallpox attack against us.

What is smallpox?

Smallpox is a highly contagious disease caused by the variola virus, which is an orthopox virus in the same family as monkey-pox, mousepox, camelpox, rabbitpox, and cowpox. Cowpox is used to make smallpox vaccine, called vaccinia.

Smallpox no longer exists as a naturally occurring disease, having been wiped out by the World Health Organization's (WHO) worldwide smallpox eradication program in the 1960s and '70s. But, for thousands of years, since it first appeared about 12,000 years ago in settlements in northeast Africa, smallpox had been one of the most feared plagues, killing hundreds of millions of people, decimating whole civilizations, and not even sparing kings. The mummy of the great Egyptian pharaoh Ramses V, who died in 1156 B.C., bears the distinctive smallpox scarring on his face, and the Roman Emperor Marcus Aurelius was killed by smallpox in a plague that killed millions in the Roman Empire about 180 A.D. In the last decades of the 18th century, smallpox killed 400,000 Europeans a year, including four reigning monarchs, and in the 20th century the disease killed an estimated 300-500 million people. By comparison, wars in the 20th century, which was history's bloodiest century for warfare, killed 111 million people.

Historically, smallpox has killed 30% of its victims, although that number has been higher in very susceptible populations. The New World populations of Indians had never experienced smallpox, so were very susceptible. Between 1580 and 1620, smallpox reduced the Aztec population of Mexico from about 20 million to less than 2 million, after Spanish conquistadors had inadvertently introduced it there, and smallpox is the main suspect in reducing the overall North American Indian population from about 100 million at the time of Columbus's arrival to about 10 million a mere 50 years later.

How is it spread?

Smallpox is normally spread through direct contact with an infected person, and transmission of the virus occurs when a person inhales a virus-containing airborne droplet of an infected person's saliva. But it can also spread from contact with an infected person's fluids, clothing, and bedding. It is not spread by animals or insects.

The virus is very stable and will survive for months in an infected person's clothing and bedding, even dried in the dust in his sick room, in the form of viral material from the smallpox pustules or from the pustules' crusted scabs. These are much less infectious than the airborne droplets, but infected clothing and bed linens have historically been a source of smallpox outbreaks in Europe.

Smallpox victims are infectious with the onset of rash, which occurs 2-4 days after the onset of fever, which occurs 10-14 days after initial exposure to the disease. Victims are most infectious during the initial week (after development of rash) when they develop lesions in the mucous membranes of the mouth, tongue,

212

larynx, pharynx, and upper part of the esophagus. The victim sheds part of the lesions in airborne water droplets during this period. As the lesions develop on the skin, the person remains infectious to a declining degree until the lesions turn to scabs and the scabs fall off.

Types of smallpox

There are three types of smallpox, ordinary, flat, and hemorrhagic, that can occur in unvaccinated persons, plus a fourth type, modified, that can occur in previously vaccinated people.

1) Ordinary smallpox (Variola major): This is by far the most common type. Once exposed to ordinary smallpox, it takes from 7-17 days for symptoms to appear. (The average incubation time is 12-14 days.) Then, symptoms are flu-like, progressing from a high fever, cough, and fatigue to headache, backache, and other body aches with occasional vomiting and disorientation. After 2-4 days of these symptoms, the fever peaks and begins to decline, ushering in a rash that develops into hard painful lesions. The lesions appear first on the mucous membranes and pharynx, then on the face, forearms, and hands. Within a day or two, the trunk and lower limbs, including the palms of the hands and soles of the feet, also become involved with the rash. The rash lasts for about two weeks and becomes most pronounced on the face, forearms, and lower legs. At the end of 14 days, the lesions, which by now have developed into hard-raised painful sores called pustules, begin to dry up and crust over. By about day 19, the scabs begin falling off, with the scabs on the palms and soles falling off last. The resulting scars, which are most pronounced on the face, are the result of the destruction of the underlying sebaceous glands.

Thirty percent of victims will die, usually from toxemia leading to respiratory or heart failure. Death, if it occurs, is usually in the second week. Some victims will also become blind, generally as a result of opportunistic bacterial infections.

Ordinary smallpox can sometimes be confused with chickenpox. With chickenpox, however, the rash is more uniformly distributed on the body, with no rash on the palms or soles.

2) Flat type smallpox: This is very rare and is believed associated with a deficient immune system. It occurs more frequently in children and is characterized by intense toxemia. The lesions remain soft and velvety, and never progress to the pustular stage. Although the majority of cases are fatal, survivors typically are not scarred.

3) Hemorrhagic smallpox: This is also rare and associated with people with a compromised immune system. It occurs more frequently in adults. The virus multiplies in the spleen and bone marrow and leads to the inability of the blood to clot, resulting in spontaneous bleeding from spots on the skin and from the mucous membranes. The illness includes a shortened incubation period followed by severe high fever, headache, and stomach pain. These victims are highly infectious, and death occurs in the fifth or sixth day after incubation, before lesions typical of ordinary smallpox have a chance to develop.

4) Modified type smallpox: This type usually appears in previously vaccinated people. The incubation period, followed by headache and body pains, are similar to ordinary smallpox. The rash, however, develops without the presence of fever, and lesions are fewer, more superficial, and progress more quickly, with crusting accomplished within 10 days. These victims are infec-

tious, but not nearly as infectious as victims with ordinary smallpox.

History of smallpox vaccine

The decision by President Bush to resume smallpox vaccination marks the first time in U.S. history that a nationwide public health preventive measure has been put into operation to defend against attack with disease.

The vaccine for smallpox is called vaccinia. It is a live virus derived from cowpox, a relative of smallpox but much milder.

The earliest form of smallpox inoculation was developed in China and India about 1000 B.C. Called variolation, it consisted of taking the pus from the pox of an infected person and inoculating a healthy person with it. A mild form of the virus developed and granted the person lifelong immunity. The practice spread to Europe and the New World in the 1700s.

In Britain in the mid 1700s, cowpox was a disease that primarily affected milkmaids, and it was noticed that they became resistant to smallpox after they recovered. In 1774, a British farmer from Dorset inoculated his family with material taken from the udders of a cow with cowpox, thereby granting his family immunity from smallpox. And in 1796 a British surgeon extracted fluid from the pustule of a cowpox victim and injected it into a healthy child, conferring smallpox protection on him. By 1800, smallpox vaccination campaigns using cowpox began throughout Europe.

Modern science has now learned that cowpox is a virus that primarily infects rodents and only occasionally infects cows. It exists primarily in Europe.

The World Health Organization's (WHO) worldwide smallpox vaccination program, designed to eradicate the disease, began in

1967 and ended in 1980 when smallpox was officially declared eradicated, making it the only human disease ever eradicated. The last reported case of smallpox was in Somalia in 1971, and in the United States the last reported case was in 1949. Vaccinations for U.S. civilians stopped in 1972, and U.S. military smallpox vaccinations stopped in 1990. Vaccine production discontinued in the U.S. in 1982.

When eradicated, the world community agreed to keep two samples of the disease in laboratory repositories in the United States at the CDC in Atlanta, and in the Soviet Union at the Russian State Research Center of Virology and Biotechnology in Koltsovo, Novosibirsk, which is in central Siberia.

Vaccination has begun again under a renewed threat of the return of the disease. It is feared that hostile states such as Iraq and North Korea, and possibly terrorists like Al Qaida, now have the smallpox virus and may use it against us. The threat has become more credible since the terrorist attacks in New York on September 11, 2001 and the subsequent anthrax attack by an unknown person or persons shortly thereafter.

Types of vaccines and availability

There is currently enough smallpox vaccine to vaccinate all 288.6 million residents of the U.S. This includes about 75 million doses of the 1970s-era Dryvax vaccine and about 300 million doses of the 1950s-era Wetvax vaccine. The old vaccine has been stored cold and has been tested every two or three years to gauge its potency. Some of the vaccine has been diluted up to five times to make it go further, but tests indicate it is still potent.

The U.S. has ordered 209 million more doses of a more modern smallpox vaccine from Acambis Inc., a Cambridge,

Massachusetts-based company, and it should be ready for use in early 2004. It hasn't been fully tested, but initial tests indicate it will be safe and effective. The FDA has not yet licensed enough of any of the vaccine for general public use, but it will be made available to the public without licensing in the event of a small-pox epidemic emergency. There is no definitive way to test the potency and safety of the new vaccine in the absence of an out-break of smallpox.

Protection

Successful vaccination produces total immunity to smallpox. Once vaccinated, it takes approximately 7-10 days to achieve protection. However, if you are vaccinated within 3-4 days of ini-tial exposure to smallpox, you may receive total protection from the disease, or at least protection against severe illness. The vac-cine is then good for about 5-10 years (no one knows for sure). If you are later revaccinated, it is believed immunity from smallpox lasts even longer, although how long no one knows. There is no danger in being vaccinated multiple times. Dr. D.A. Henderson, the director for the Center for Civilian Bio-Defense Studies at Johns Hopkins University, who in 1966 was the WHO director overseeing the global eradication of smallpox, says he has been vaccinated between 25 and 100 times. The live vaccinia virus vaccine, he says, must grow in your skin to produce immunity to smallpox. If you are already sufficiently immune, the vaccine simply does not grow in the skin.

The severity of lesions from smallpox can vary greatly, either naturally or because vaccination years before has given a person partial, but not complete, protection. With nearly complete pro-tection from vaccine, few lesions will appear, but even if a person was vaccinated many years before, lesions may be far less and more superficial than for a person who was never vaccinated. In this case, a person could get a mild case of smallpox, with an accompanying mild rash. He will not die and may not even get very sick, but he may be contagious, capable of passing along full-blown smallpox to another person.

Adverse reactions to vaccine

Smallpox vaccine has a higher adverse reaction rate than any of the modern vaccines generally given. Based on the statistics of the 1960s and '70s smallpox eradication program, as many as 50% of people being vaccinated will have some sort of reaction from the vaccine, ranging from a sore, swollen arm and swollen glands to flu-like symptoms. In a study of adult primary vaccinees, it was determined that 36% became sufficiently ill to miss school, work, or a recreational activity, or to have trouble sleeping. In another study, 17% had fever of at least 100 degrees Fahrenheit within two weeks of vaccination, 7% had a fever of 100 degrees or more, and 1.4% had a fever of 102 degrees or more.

One or two of every million people who get the vaccine for the first time will die from it, 15-50 will have life threatening reactions, including eczema vaccinatum, progressive vaccinia (vaccinia necrosum), and post-vaccinal encephalitis, and approximately 1,000 will have serious reactions, including a toxic or allergic reaction at the vaccine site and spread of the vaccinia virus to other parts of the body. If all 130 million Americans never vaccinated got vaccinated, about 250 would die and 2,000 would have life-threatening reactions. This does not include people with AIDS, who could be very severely affected.

218

The data showed that the death rate and adverse reaction rate for those being revaccinated was cut by two-thirds, but still if all 158 million Americans who were previously vaccinated were to get revaccinated, it is expected that 40 would die and 800 would have life-threatening reactions. Again, this does not take into account people with AIDS or other immune system problems.

Compare these adverse reaction rates with a more modern vaccine such as the measles/mumps/rubella vaccine, which has experienced 11 adverse reactions and no deaths among the 30 million people vaccinated in the last 12 years. The newer smallpox vaccine, the 209 million doses still under final testing, is expected to have fewer adverse reactions than the older smallpox vaccine.

The death rate and adverse reaction rate may be much higher today because the U.S. population, or any modern population, is highly susceptible to smallpox because it has been so long (1949) since the disease has been present in the U.S. and because it has been so long (1972) since vaccinations were discontinued. Health officials expect the death and adverse reaction rate to be much lower among that older 58% of our population that has been vaccinated in the past, even though for most of them it has been the distant past, and they expect the adverse reactions in the younger 42% of the population never vaccinated at all to be significantly higher.

The most frequent complications

From previous data, adverse reactions from vaccination occurred most often in people receiving their first dose of the vaccine, and among children under the age of 5. Following are the most frequent complications:

1) Inadvertent inoculation at other sites: This accounted for half of all complications of vaccination. Occurring in 1 of every 2,000 primary inoculations, it generally resulted from the hand touching the vaccination site, then touching another part of the body, thereby transferring the vaccination. The most frequent inadvertent inoculations occurred on the mouth, eyelid, rectum, genitals, nose, and face. It generally resolves itself.

2) Generalized vaccinia: This occurred in 1 of every 5,000 primary vaccinations, and it is the result of blood-borne dissemination of vaccinia virus. It generally resolves itself unless there is an underlying condition involving an immune deficiency. Vaccinia Immune Globulin (VIG) (see Sidebar) can be used to successfully treat cases involving the eye.

3) Eczema vaccinatum: This occurred in 1 out of every 26,000 primary vaccinations, and it occurred in people who had current or healed eczema or other chronic skin problems. It typically covers the area affected by the skin condition, and it is usually mild and resolves itself. But, on occasion it can be severe or fatal. VIG is used to successfully treat serious cases.

4) Progressive vaccinia (vaccinia necrosum): This is rare, severe, and often fatal, and it is caused by the vaccine site's failure to heal. It occurs in people with underlying immune disorders and can occur after primary vaccination or revaccination. VIG is used to treat it, but with varying success.

5) Post-vaccination encephalitis: Also rare, this occurred in 1 out of 300,000 cases of primary vaccinations, with most occurring in children under the age of one year. It is characterized by fever, headache, vomiting, and sometimes convulsions, paralysis, or coma. Symptoms manifest themselves 8-15 days after vacci-

nation. About 15-25% of cases died and another 25% had permanent neurological damage. VIG is not effective.

Voluntary vaccination and "herd immunity"

A survey of Americans in late 2002 indicated that more than half of Americans would be willing to get vaccinated. But the survey was taken before there was widespread understanding of the risks involved.

At present, the vaccine is being made available only to the military and the 10 million or so emergency health care "first responders" such as police, firefighters, ambulance crews, EMTs, hospital emergency care workers, etc. When the vaccine is made available to the public, it will be on a voluntary basis. People will simply have to weigh the risk of having an adverse reaction against the risk that we will be attacked with smallpox. The idea of making it widely available on a volunteer basis is to build up "herd immunity." Since a certain number of people will opt for the vaccine, the nation's "herd immunity" will increase. Then, if we are attacked with smallpox, the increased herd immunity will lessen the severity of any resulting epidemic.

In the event of a smallpox epidemic, the Centers for Disease Control and Prevention (CDC) recommends everyone get vaccinated, even if you have AIDS. The risk of getting smallpox far outweighs the risk of having an adverse reaction from the vaccine. The vaccine can be taken for up to four days after exposure to smallpox and still be effective in either preventing the disease or greatly lessening its effects.

Although the CDC says smallpox vaccination will be on a voluntary basis, it is anticipated that in the event of an attack and subsequent smallpox epidemic, smallpox vaccinations will likely become mandatory in affected areas. Quarantines and isolation will definitely be mandatory. Based on historical experience, there is no other way to contain an epidemic.

You won't be able to sue

If you are one of the unlucky ones who does get an adverse reaction to the vaccine, you won't be able to sue anyone. The Homeland Security Act has a provision protecting vaccine makers and health care providers from such suits. People injured may sue in federal court, but they will have to prove negligence, which will be just about impossible because the vaccine is advertised as coming with risks. The liability protection for vaccine makers was deemed necessary in light of the fact the U.S. needed a new vaccine fast and no company was willing to make one unless they got liability protection.

Genetically altered smallpox

All of the above may become moot if we are attacked with a genetically altered form of of the smallpox virus. No one knows if such a virus exists, but Soviet defector Dr. Ken Alibek, the former chief scientist and first deputy director of Biopreparat, the former Soviet Union's secret offensive bioweapons program, says the Soviet Union was working on such a virus when he left their program in 1992. Dr Alibek is now a U.S. citizen and chief scientist at a private company in the U.S. that specializes in researching and developing medical defenses against biological weapons.

Also, both NBC News and the *New York Times* have reported that another former Russian virologist, the late Dr. Nelja Maltseva, may have given the genetically altered strain of smallpox to Iraq.

Researchers have tested their ability to alter a related orthopox virus. They inserted the gene interleukin-4 into the mousepox virus, then exposed mice previously vaccinated against mousepox to the genetically altered virus. As they feared, many of the mice died. They are not sure if a genetically altered smallpox virus would defeat the smallpox vaccine, but it is definitely a fear.

The Iraq connection

Before they were thrown out in 1998, U.N. inspectors had discovered that Iraq had experimented with camelpox, another relative of smallpox, and one fear is that camelpox, which ordinarily does not harm humans, might be modified and used as a biological weapon. The smallpox vaccine, however, protects against all orthopox viruses, including camelpox. During their inspections in Iraq, U.N. inspectors found a freeze-drier labeled smallpox. Also, after the first Gulf War, 69 Iraqi prisoners of war were blood tested and were found to have built up immunity to smallpox, indicating prior vaccination against the disease. The obvious question is, why?

Genetically engineered vaccines and anti-viral agents

U.S. scientists, meanwhile, are working on a genetically engineered vaccine that will be more effective with fewer side effects than old vaccines. They are also working on anti-viral agents that could, for the first time in history, effectively treat a person already infected with smallpox. No one knows if these efforts will be successful any time soon, but early laboratory studies suggest the drug cidofovir may be effective. Tests with animals are ongoing and being monitored by the CDC and NIH. There are 3,500 doses of cidofovir on hand at present, which is enough to handle anticipated reactions if 15 million people are vaccinated.

It will be administered under an investigational new drug proto-col. Otherwise, there is no treatment beyond intravenous fluids and medicines to control pain and secondary infections.

Sidebars

The ring method of stopping a smallpox outbreak

At present, the Centers for Disease Control's (CDC) plan to contain a smallpox attack includes widespread voluntary vacci-nation but, if necessary, forced quarantine of infected individuals and mandatory tracing and vaccination of anyone who may have come in contact with them.

They will employ the "ring" method to control an epidemic, namely vaccinate everyone who has had contact with an infected person, then vaccinate the ring of people who have had contact with the first set of contacts. It's the method used so successfully in the 1960s and '70s to finally eradicate smallpox.

Keep in mind that for up to four days after exposure to small-pox, vaccination will either keep a person from catching the dis-ease or lessen its severity.

Vaccinia Immune Globulin

A major difficulty in treating adverse reactions to the vaccine is that in past years bad reactions were treated with Vaccinia Immune Globulin (VIG), which is serum derived from people who recovered from infection with the vaccine virus. Due to the absence of smallpox vaccinations for 30-plus years, the supply of VIG is now about 700 doses, which is enough for anticipated adverse reactions if only 6 million people get vaccinated. Additional doses of VIG are being produced.

People who should not be vaccinated

1) Eczema, dermatitis: People who have had or now have atopic dermatitis or eczema should not get the vaccine unless they are exposed to smallpox. As many as 40 million Americans, or up to 15% of the population, have had or currently have eczema, which puts them at higher risk for a potentially fatal skin infection called eczema vaccinatum. The risk is particularly great for children, who have experienced a threefold increase in eczema since smallpox vaccination ended three decades ago. In a study from the 1970s, 123 people out of one million vaccinated people got eczema vaccinatum, most of them children. In another study in Europe, 6% of people infected with eczema vaccinatum died from it. Running the numbers, if the 40 million Americans suspected of having had or currently having eczema were to get the vaccine, the death toll among them would be 295.

2) AIDS, other immune deficiency disorders: People who have a suppressed immune system, such as people who have had transplants or who have cancer, leukemia, lymphoma, or people with HIV and AIDS, are high-risk groups. AIDS was not a known disease when vaccinations were given 30 years ago, so the severity of reaction for people with AIDS is not clear. Side effects can include brain swelling and extensive toxicity. Of particular concern to health authorities are the 100,000 to 350,000 Americans who have AIDS but who don't know it. Also, if you are taking immune suppressive medications such as corticosteroids, or if you are undergoing radiation, you should not be vaccinated.

3) Pregnant women, children: Pregnant women should not be vaccinated, nor should they be vaccinated if they plan to get

pregnant within one month of vaccination. Infants should also not get the vaccine.

The current recommendation that infants not be vaccinated is in sharp contrast to the smallpox vaccination programs of the 1960s and '70s, when most of the vaccinations were given to children under the age of 1. Now, children under the age of one year are considered at increased risk for vaccine-caused brain infection. Children have been omitted from all of the current studies involving smallpox vaccines. Because children are more prone to touching the vaccination site, then touching other parts of their bodies such as their eyes, or even touching other children, the vaccination site should be covered with a special extra sticky bandage.

Also, if you have any of the following conditions, you should not get the vaccine until you have completely healed: Burns, shingles, impetigo, herpes, severe acne or psoriasis, and chickenpox.

Since the vaccinia vaccine is a live virus and can accidentally spread to others, causing inadvertent vaccination, those people living with any of the above at-risk people should not be vaccinated. A vaccinated person is infectious until the vaccination site scabs over. A vaccinated person could spread the vaccinia virus by touching the vaccination site, then touching another person. In the '60s and '70s it was common for this to happen among young siblings.

In all, about 50 million Americans should not get the vaccine, either because they have one of the conditions mentioned above or because they live with someone who does.

How vaccine is given

The vaccine is given by dipping a bifurcated (two-pronged) needle into the vaccine, then puncturing the skin of the upper arm 15 times in a few seconds. The puncturing of the skin is not deep. If the vaccination is successful, within 3-4 days a red, itchy bump will form, then develop into a large blister that fills with pus and drains. In two weeks, the blister dries up and a scab forms. The scab falls off in the third week and leaves a small scar. To prevent the vaccinia virus in the vaccine from spreading to other people or other parts of your body, the vaccine site should be covered with a bandage. Children especially should be watched so they do not touch the site, then inadvertently touch, say, their eye.

Guns and crime

The burglar does far more than steal!

(originally published in September 2004)

"Never mind about stealing the damn stuff!

This is the wrong place!

We have to leave!"

"That's what they were saying Dad, right outside my window," my 12-year-old son Jake told me as I tried to shake the last remnants of sleep from my brain.

"They were just there," he insisted.

It was 6:30 a.m., and I had gone to bed late. I was really tired. "You probably had a dream, Jake," I told him.

"No, Dad, it was for real! They were right outside my window! Then they ran down the driveway!"

Suddenly, Lenie called to me in a near panicky voice from the living room: "Dave, they were in the house! The window is wide open! There are chairs pulled up to it!"

I walked the 20 feet or so from my bed to the open living room window and sat on a chair. There's an explanation for all this, I thought to myself. Jake had a dream, and the window is open, and chairs moved for a reason. It will come to me as soon as I clear my head.

It dawned on me slowly that morning that we had been burgled, as we slept, and it took me a half hour to call the sheriff because

I just couldn't believe it could happen way out here in this beautiful Oregon countryside, with my Black Lab either asleep or silently witnessing the whole thing, with my wife and I asleep 20 feet away from the open window they used.

Astonishing! Even six weeks later it's astonishing. I've accepted the burglary, but I still can hardly believe that I and my damn dog slept through it. What if I had been awoken by a desperate burglar with a gun or a knife to my throat? What if they had harmed my children, whose bedrooms were in the other end of the house, where Jake had heard them talking right outside his bedroom window?

They had taken nothing, as far as we can tell. The sheriff's department surmised they had hit the wrong house, didn't know there were people at home, and may have been after my neighbor's medical marijuana stash. His house is just up the road, but has a difficult long driveway to navigate for people not used to going there. The burglars may have simply picked my driveway by mistake.

Although nothing was taken, my notebook computer was on the floor, and a subsequent examination of it revealed the liquid plasma screen was damaged, as if a big dog like my 80-pound Lab had stepped on it. Reconstructing the burglary, I am assuming the notebook computer got accidentally knocked on the floor, then my dog stepped on the screen as she went over, tail wagging, to greet the thieves. Did you know Labs are very friendly dogs?

I've taken several steps since the burglary to prevent its reoccurrence, including getting a second dog that barks when it's supposed to. I'm teaching my children the basics of shooting, and my wife, Ilene, will take a concealed-carry course with my daughter and a neighbor lady. And I practice with my .45 and folding stock

Mini-14 far more often than I had prior to the burglary. Plus, I carry concealed at all times.

What I haven't done yet is mentally recover from the fact that my family and I could have been at the mercy of criminals in my own house. I can't shake that dread in the back of my mind that, although I had never been burgled or victimized by a crime before in my 60 years of life, now I was vulnerable. I wasn't even awake to defend my family when things could have been desperate for them.

Burglars do far more harm than steal your stuff. They steal your security. They violate your home, plunder your personal space. They steal certainty and replace it with uncertainty. They take the future you worked so hard to build and make it more tenuous. When you try to go to sleep at night, the burglar is there whispering, "I might be back tonight!"

Every night I go through my checklist: Doors and windows locked, gun within reach, bedroom door cracked a bit so I can hear my children in case they call for help. But I am not as confident going to sleep anymore, and ask myself foreboding questions: Will I waken and reach for my gun in time? Are the doors and windows locked sufficiently, or do criminals have clever means of bypassing any locks? Have my children unwittingly unlocked a window at the other end of the house, where they will have to face a crazed intruder alone before I can get there?"

Burglars, and all criminals whose deeds risk violence, destroy parts of society. They are like arsonists, setting little fires all over the place, burning down what the rest of us try to build up. We build hope for the future, and they burn it down. I hope all you burglars in prison, some of whom probably subscribe to this magazine, realize what you've done to your victims and to society as a whole. It's not the simple matter that you stole some stuff that your victim's insurance will replace, anyway. You stole part of their life, and by extension destroyed part of this great land called America that the rest of us try to improve by our hard work and dedication to our families. You deserve prison.

From a strictly nuts-and-bolts security standpoint, the burglary at my house was a cheap wakeup call. I had grown a little too lax about the locks and guns I own for self protection. I'm now more diligent. I've installed safeguards, and I'm in a heightened state of alertness and readiness. I'll be awake the next time, and ready! So will other members of my family.

But I miss that carefree feeling the burglars stole.

Let's stop apologizing for guns

(originally published in March 2000)

I carry a concealed Ruger P97 .45 caliber eight-shot semi-automatic handgun almost everywhere I go, and I keep a Ruger Mini-14 semi-automatic rifle with folding stock in my home within easy reach. The ammunition clips of both hold bullets designed to kill a violent criminal instantaneously, before he can take another step or move his hand another inch. I don't keep gun locks on these weapons, and I don't apologize for them. And it's not just because it is my Constitutional right to keep guns, although that is reason enough. It is because I have been convinced by overwhelming evidence that guns keep me and my family safe.

Does that sound like the rantings of a paranoid, gun-toting nut? Probably, if you are a paranoid, gun-grabbing ignoramus who knows nothing about guns and the role they play daily in American society in the prevention of crime. To those of you who do know the relationship of gun and crime statistics, the weapons I keep probably make a lot of sense.

We who own guns for self-protection have been much maligned by those who think guns are evil, even though the statistics about gun use show that guns are used far more often by average citizens to prevent violent crime than they are used by criminals to commit crimes. Now the evidence is greater than ever, thanks to the largest and most accurate study ever undertaken. It was performed by John Lott, a senior research scholar at Yale Law School who had never owned a gun and who had spent most of his career doing research on nongun-related issues. The study's findings are contained in his scholarly 1998 book, *More Guns, Less Crime* (University of Chicago Press), which is a detailed analysis of 18 years of the gun/crime relationship in all 3,000-plus counties in the United States. After Lott finished the study, he went out and bought his first gun.

Here are a few of the things he found, much of which will sound like plain common sense to us gun owners:

• In counties that have "right-to-carry" laws or "shall-issue" permits, that is, where a citizen must be issued a gun permit after meeting certain criteria, usually a background check and having taken a gun safety course, violent crime goes down dramatically while it goes up in surrounding counties that issue permits only at the discretion of the relevant law enforcement agency. Furthermore, the crime rate continues to go down year after year due to the increasing deterrence of more people getting the "shall-issue" permits.

• Private citizens use guns to defend themselves against criminals more than 2,000,000 times a year. Since the safety of children is often cited by gun opponents who don't want guns in private homes, the study analyzed deaths of children per year for the sake of comparison. For children under age 5 in the United States, less than 20 died of gunshot, about 100 drowned in bathtubs, and about 40 drowned in 5-gallon water buckets.

• Resistance with a gun, rather than passive resistance, is the safest option for the private citizen when confronted by a criminal. For a woman, especially, it is the best option, increasing her chances of not being injured by two and a half times.

• The biggest drops in violent crime occurred in urban areas, especially in poor neighborhoods, and among women and the elderly, who are most vulnerable.

When his study was released, Lott was instantly attacked by the likes of New York Senator Charles Schumer and other anti-gun advocates as being a stooge of the gun industry, which he is not. The mass media briefly mentioned his book, then ignored it much like they have ignored the 2,000,000 annual instances in which guns are used to prevent crime while heavily reporting the under 20 instances of young children being killed by guns.

What are we to conclude from this study, especially in the wake of the mass shootings at some of the nation's schools, such as at Columbine High School? If it is clear that guns save lives far more often than they take them, what happened at Columbine? May I be so crass and insensitive to suggest that some of the teachers should have been armed? In a country like Israel where they fear attacks by madmen and terrorists, the teachers carry guns into the classroom and they consequently have no gun attacks on their students. Here in the United States, we have a federal law that bans guns from within 1000 feet of schools, even sometimes posting signs outside the school announcing to the world and to the nuts it is a "gun-free zone." Do you think there may be an analogy here, that perhaps Israel's policy works and ours doesn't?

In the counties mentioned in Lott's study, where "shall-issue" laws are in effect, violent crime goes down, while it goes up in the surrounding counties where there are no "shall-issue" laws. Do you think there may be a connection there, too? Do you suppose that violent criminals and nuts may be figuring out where the easy prey are?

We who realize the value of guns have been very silent in the face of the all-out war on gun ownership that is currently being waged by certain politicians and the mass media. Yet, the evidence clearly shows that gun possession and "shall-issue" laws save lives. Isn't it time we stopped apologizing for our guns and spoke up?

Anti-gun groups, politicians, and the mass media regularly hide incidents and studies that portray guns favorably, and they spare no ink to tell the rare story when guns are used by criminals or by accident. Then, they pass stupid laws that endanger our children. We who know the truth about guns need to let that truth be known: Guns save lives and prevent criminal attacks. They protect our families from harm, not expose them to danger.

Freedom, guns, & boycotts

(originally published in September 2001)

The other day I walked into my local Ace Hardware store and cancelled this magazine's longstanding account.

"How come?" Dan, the owner asked surprised. I had shopped there ever since the company moved to Gold Beach, Oregon, three years ago and knew everyone firsthand.

"Ace is using Rosie O'Donnell to help sell their products," I said. "And Rosie O'Donnell wants to put me in jail because I own a gun."

"But we're apolitical," he said. "We have nothing to do with that."

"You have the Ace Hardware sign on your door," I said, "which means you benefit from their advertising."

"But, we're a family-owned business, Dave, you know that," he protested.

I felt very bad at that moment. His business was similar to mine: Just a few employees, family members working hard to keep things going. They relied on every account in this small town. But, I knew I had to make a statement at the local level in defense of the Second Amendment, which guarantees individuals like me the right to have a gun.

Rosie O'Donnell's statement when she was a spokesperson for K-Mart in 1999 was foremost in my mind: "I don't care if you think it's your right," she said, "I say: Sorry, it's 1999. We have had enough as a nation. You are not allowed to own a gun, and if you do own a gun, I think you should go to prison."

I and tens of thousands of other gun owners—just a fraction of the 80 million Americans who own guns— boycotted K-Mart, and the company subsequently dumped Rosie as a spokesperson. Now, Rosie's photo was displayed prominently on Ace Hardware's internet website under the headline: "Paint Your House 'Rosie' with Ace Paint."

Outraged e-mail suggested a boycott of Ace for their support of someone who wanted to put us gun owners in prison, and I agreed. But the boycott was more personal this time. There had been no K-Mart in Gold Beach, but my neighbor, Dan, owned the local Ace Hardware.

"It's going to be costly for me, too," I told Dan. "You're the only good hardware store in town. But there comes a time when a person has to take a step in the direction of freedom. Rosie O'Donnell wants to put me in jail, and Ace Hardware supports her. I have no choice but to fight back in the only tangible way I can—by boycotting Ace Hardware and anything connected with Ace and Rosie O'Donnell."

The owner, not understanding, waved his hand at me angrily and walked away in a huff.

Less than two days later, alarmed by the thousands of people like me who had taken similar action, Ace distanced itself from Rosie O'Donnell, closing the offending page on its website and sending out e-mails and letters to angry customers like me stating: "Ace Hardware has not and does not employ Rosie

O'Donnell as a spokesperson, nor do we have any official relationship or affiliation with her."

The boycott had taken two days, and I reopened my Ace
Hardware account. "It was all a mistake," said the grateful Dan.
"Rosie wasn't really acting as an Ace spokeswoman."

I relate this incident because it illustrates a critical lesson for all
of us who support the U.S. Constitution and its Amendments,
including and especially the Second Amendment. The power of
economic boycott is a big weapon at our disposal. We no longer
have to roll over and play dead every time some misguided but
influential gun grabber like Rosie O'Donnell tries to take away
our rights. In the face of the mass media eagerly reporting her
every word while portraying gun owners as villains, we can fight
back, quietly but with tremendous effect, by means of the economic boycott.

And let's not forget Smith and Wesson, the gun maker brought
to its knees by the economic boycott of gun owners after S&W
made a sell-out deal with the federal government to protect its
hide from lawsuits. So outraged were gun owners with S&W that
they have been slow to forgive, and S&W will likely not recover
from the loss of financial revenue.

People like Rosie O'Donnell have been given a free ride when
they try to strip us of our rights. That is a recipe for disaster for
gun owners. It's not enough that we contribute money to organizations like the NRA and GOA so that they can fight the
Congressional battles for us. We must take to the streets ourselves
in forms like the economic boycott to make Rosie and the companies that support her pay. If it means crippling them like we
have done to S&W, so be it. Remember, she wants to put us in
prison because we exercise a Constitutional right.

Rosie O'Donnell just launched a national magazine called *Rosie*. In it, she is unapologetic about her stance to imprison gun owners like you and me. In her page 2 "from rosie" column, she even frets about the difficulty of getting big advertisers to support the magazine. The big advertisers who do support her in the August issue of the magazine include Ford, Chevy, Kellogg, Clorox, Johnson & Johnson, Doubleday Book Club, and Target. I'll boycott them all, and write their main offices and tell them why.

This isn't about Rosie, it's about freedom and rights. There are 80 million of us she wants to imprison. If we don't act now, while we still have the chance, she may someday get her wish.

Postscript: The magazine, Rosie, went bankrupt, in part due to a lack of advertisers.

The real gun criminals

(originally published in May 2000)

If a person robbed a bank and murdered someone, and you drove the getaway car, would you be guilty of accessory to robbery and murder?

If a man raped a woman after you intentionally provided him the key to her home knowing his intentions, would you be guilty of accessory to rape?

The answer to both questions, as we all know, is yes, because you knowingly facilitated the commission of the crime.

Why then are not the likes of President Clinton, Senator Charles Schumer (D-NY), or Senator Dianne Feinstein (D-CA) guilty of accessory to murder and rape for their support of laws that restrict the use of firearms, since study after study clearly show that the personal possession of firearms dramatically lowers the incidence of murder and rape in America?

According to economist John Lott, author of the landmark statistical study, *More Guns, Less Crime*, restrictive gun laws are directly linked to increased murder and rape rates. Lott studied the crime rates for all U.S. counties spanning an 18-year period. He found that the highest murder and rape rates were in the counties with the most restrictive gun laws, the second highest in those with less restrictive gun laws, and the lowest in those with "right-to-carry" laws; that is, where residents had a law-protected "right to carry" a personal firearm so long as he or she met certain minimum requirements.

Thirty one states now have "right-to-carry" laws, and all of them are experiencing dramatic declines in murder and rape since the laws were enacted. The statistics indicate that if the 29 states without "right-to-carry" laws were to adopt them, at least 1,000 murders and many thousands of rapes would be prevented every year.

Can any scientific study be clearer? The evidence could not be more overwhelming. Even school shootings are all but eliminated in states that have "right-to-carry" laws. The most recent highly publicized school shootings—in Michigan where a 6-year-old girl was shot to death by a classmate, and at Colorado's Columbine High School—took place in states that do not have "right-to-carry" laws.

Although other countries were not studied by Lott, the data is already coming in: Disarmed Australia and England are both experiencing an explosion in violent crime, while armed-to-the-teeth Israel and Switzerland are experiencing little crime and no school shootings.

Lott's definitive study is known to Clinton, Schumer, and Feinstein, as well as to other anti-gun politicians, members of the mass media, Handgun Control Inc., and all the other groups who want to ban guns and disarm American citizens. But they continue to dance on the graves of the latest shooting victims, using their bodies as platforms to launch ever more calls to ban ever more guns. They tout their blatantly false anti-gun dogma, knowing full-well that the truth about gun statistics makes them liars and accessories to murders and rapes.

Their friends in the mass media are just as guilty. They make sure each shooting at a school or restaurant becomes a high profile media event so the politicians can spout their lies, but the media deliberately ignores the two million times per year a crime is prevented by a private citizen using his or her personal firearm. In the vast majority of cases, the would-be victim merely has to brandish the gun to stop the crime, but every year there are many women who shoot down their would-be rapists just in time and others who shoot down their would-be murderers just in time. But the unarmed ones are often raped and murdered.

Why are not these lying members of the media also charged with being an accessory to murder and rape, along with our lying politicians? People like Clinton, Schumer, and Feinstein don't care that their statements are false. They don't even care if they are later corrected by someone armed with the facts, because they know that the corrections will get little play in the mass media while their initial distortions will get repeated again and again. These politicians and their media allies are deliberately distorting the truth to advance their anti-gun ideology. To them, our children are merely pawns in this ideological struggle. If a few of them get killed because of their distortions, so what!

Why do we let these people get away with their lies when it is our children and our friends who are being murdered and raped? Hypocrite Feinstein is responsible for California's very restrictive gun law, which makes it next to impossible to get a permit to carry a concealed handgun. But on the sly she has obtained a concealed handgun permit for herself. What gall! She knows how to be safe, and she wants to protect her own butt and let us and our families take our chances of becoming a victim of her law—all in the name of her anti-gun ideology.

People like Clinton, Schumer, and Feinstein don't fight on ground that tries to explore the truth. They fight on ideological grounds—their ideology of a disarmed America where only the government has guns.

And let us not forget what history teaches us about a disarmed nation where only the government has guns. It has ushered in every tyranny of the last hundred years, from Hitler's Nazi Germany to Stalin's Communist Soviet Union—so the government can enforce its ideology on the rest of us.

Which brings up a final question: Why are we letting this happen?

Personal guns getting to be in style

(originally published in March 2002)

Have you noticed how the mass media's attacks against gun ownership have gone way down since the terrorist attacks of September 11? Of course, it's kind of difficult to continue an unrelenting assault against gun ownership when half of your readers are going out and buying handguns to protect their families against terrorists.

Some in the media are even reporting incidents in which law-abiding citizens have used personal firearms to defend themselves against criminals. In one recent robbery in Dorchester, a Boston neighborhood I lived in for three years, a liquor store clerk pulled out his own personal handgun after three robbers shot and stabbed two fellow clerks. The clerk, Kenneth Hoang, 31, shot all three robbers, who then fled only to be arrested a short while later while sitting in a pool of blood and stolen money.

What is amazing is that the story was actually written up in the *Boston Globe*, one of the more anti-gun newspapers in America's overwhelmingly anti-gun mass media. After ignoring the estimated 2½ million cases last year of private citizens using guns to stop crimes, the *Globe* finally reports one.

Wow! The September 11 attacks changed even more things than I thought.

Of course, the *Globe* did put some editorial comment into the story they wrote, calling the incident a "rare act of urban defiance" and quoting an anti-gun zealot: "I'm glad that it worked out in this particular case. But in the future we may be looking at a tragedy."

Tragedy? The tragedy is that it took the *Boston Globe* so long to take off its ideological blinders and finally report an incident that shows guns are so frequently put to good use. The tragedy is that the mass media across the nation has heretofore ignored the 2½ million annual cases of self-defense successes using personal firearms, but has laid in wait for the rare school shooting so they could plaster it all over their front pages for weeks.

Statistics compiled by law enforcement show the increased personal possession of firearms lowers violent crime in direct proportion to the amount of increase. Example: In the 33 states that now permit its residents to carry concealed handguns, the violent crime rate has dropped dramatically—up to 13% in the largest counties studied. Conversely, in England, where draconian laws banning handguns were passed in 1997, violent crime is up 40%. Disarmed Australia is having the same problems as England, while armed-to-the-teeth Israel and Switzerland are experiencing low violent crime rates.

Until recently, however, the mass media not only refused to report studies showing guns in a favorable light, but they actively campaigned against gun ownership, using bogus statistics manufactured by outfits like Handgun Control, Inc. Now, since September 11, they're not only reporting incidents of private citizens defending themselves with firearms, but a lot of reporters are going out themselves and buying handguns.

I never thought I'd see the day: Personal guns for self-protection are getting to be in vogue. Gun stores can barely keep guns in stock. I'll bet gun-banning politicians like Dianne Feinstein are sure glad they already have their concealed-carry permits. It's a long line to get one now, and gun instructors are reporting that their classes are all filled up well in advance.

You know what I think? I think the news media may have just had an epiphany. They saw the attacks of September 11 and realized the nation had just been mugged, and it's time to start defending ourselves. So they collectively threw their next batch of anti-gun stories in the wastebasket and decided to write some facts about an obvious method of self-defense for America, both collectively and personally.

Ironic, isn't it? We who have always championed guns for the "freedom protectors" they are, are now joined in combat by our archenemy—the antigun liberal, gun-grabbing mass media that has tried to disarm us for years.

Maybe I should have anticipated this. Maybe it's not so astonishing after all. Maybe it was more gradual than I think. Maybe the mass media was simply the last group of people in America to finally catch on.

After all, prior to 1987, almost no state had laws allowing private citizens to carry concealed handguns, but today 33 states have such laws. The number of people applying for those permits has been increasing steadily over the years, with applications during the past year alone increasing by more than 20%.

Overwhelmingly, courts have been ruling in favor of guns, tossing out the bogus state suits against gun manufacturers one after the other. The nation's new attorney general, John Ashcroft, who is the chief law enforcement officer in the nation, is an unabashed supporter of an individual's right to own firearms.

In spite of the past silence of the mass media, the public has been making its will apparent. Gun ownership is now at an all-time high in America, while violent crime is lower than it has been in more than 10 years. Handgun Control, Inc., now known as the Brady Campaign to Prevent Gun Violence—an oxymoron if I ever heard one—has laid off 20% of its staff due to a severe downturn in contributions.

What do the cops think of all this? More than 90% say individuals should be allowed to own a personal gun for sporting or self-defense purposes, and more than 60% favor a national concealed gun carry law.

Those statistics were actually reported in the *Boston Globe*! It is indeed a new day.

Politics

Questions I'm not supposed to ask

(originally published in January 2003)

What's wrong with black Americans?

Provocative question, isn't it, especially when it's being asked by a white guy like me. We white guys aren't supposed to question what blacks do, because it automatically makes us a racist. Which brings up another obvious question: How come blacks can criticize whites, calling them honkies and racists at the drop of a hat, but whites can't criticize blacks?

Let me break my first question down into some smaller, more obvious questions:

How come when Harry Belafonte recently called Secretary of State Colin Powell "a house slave" for serving in the Bush administration, few blacks came to Powell's defense? Is it because they resented Powell's heroic climb from the slums of New York to chairman of the Joint Chiefs of Staff, then to the inner circle of the White House, without asking for any special treatment along the way?

How about when Congress was interrogating Clarence Thomas some years back during his confirmation hearings for the Supreme Court. When a lone woman accused Thomas of sexual impropriety, black leaders joined in the attack with a fury. But later, when Clinton was accused of the same thing and worse, by many women with many corroborating witnesses, blacks came to Clinton's defense? When Thomas was exonerated and confirmed, his accuser, Anita Hill, went on the speaking circuit for years attacking Justice Thomas, but few blacks criticized her. Clinton was impeached over his improprieties, but just the other day he became the first white man to be inducted into the Arkansas Black Hall of Fame as an honorary member.

What gives? Is it because Clarence Thomas was another black heroic figure who broke ranks and rose to the pinnacles of the justice system by his own determination and hard work, and Clinton has always been the white crusader wanting ever more free federal dollars for downtrodden blacks?

How about the O.J. Simpson affair? Simpson brutally murdered two innocent people. DNA tests proved it, and overwhelming evidence proved it. Yet a mainly black jury voted him "not guilty," and we all witnessed the TV scenes of crowds of blacks cheering wildly when the verdict was announced. Did they cheer because Simpson had killed two whites and got away with it? Sure looked like it!

Why did 85% of black congressmen vote against America going to war with Iraq 10 years ago, and why do Congressional blacks now hold rallies against us going to war with Iraq again? They claim it's because blacks represent a larger percentage of the armed forces so it is they who will be asked to die. But I think that's just cover for the real reason, namely that they think America is the villain in this showdown. They empathize with Iraq as the underdog, just as they perceive themselves as the underdog in America. It's America they distrust, not Iraq.

And here's a really racist question: Why haven't blacks assimilated completely into American society, even after the federal government has spent more than $700 billion on the poor—largely on poor blacks—since former President Lyndon Johnson vastly expanded welfare with his War on Poverty nearly 40 years ago? Irish people like me have assimilated, and my immigrant ancestors were valued below slaves when they arrived on the boats in places like New York and New Orleans at the height of their great flight from Irish hunger a century ago. And millions of Mexicans are assimilating right before our eyes. Is it really because racism continues to keep blacks down, or is it their own fault, a fault that mainly has to do with their desire—or lack of it—to stand on their own two feet?

These are all terrible questions for a white man to ask, I know. I must indeed be a racist to bring these things up.

But I can't help it. When I watch Colin Powell, one of the greatest Americans of my lifetime, being viciously attacked by activists like Belafonte, with people like Jesse Jackson and Spike Lee joining in, I feel like screaming: "What are you fools doing?"

Powell is a black man who has lived the American Dream. He didn't do it with the federal handouts that have done nothing for blacks but make them a permanent underclass in America. He did it by himself. Why aren't you rising in outrage against Belafonte and the rest of the attackers? Isn't this what the War on Poverty was all about, to make sure poor people, especially poor black people, could take part in the American Dream?

Of course we all, in our bitter, racist, heart of hearts, know the answer to all my questions. Black heroes like Colin Powell and Clarence Thomas believe in the wrong ideology. They believe in self-reliance. They are renegades from a liberal ideology that says blacks can't take care of themselves. Rather than criticize those blacks who have made themselves a success, blacks should feel ashamed that they, as a race, have wandered in the wilderness from one type of slavery only to find another: The new nanny state of black slavery, with Jesse Jackson and a host of white bureaucrats directing how all the welfare freebies are to be divided up. But step out of line, as Powell and Thomas did, and they'll be after your ass with a vengeance, accusing you of every crime in the book and calling you the white man's house slave. That's about as ironic as it gets!

My Irish immigrant mother has some advice for black Americans: She gave it to me in the 1950s when I was a boy in all-Irish South Boston. I had been boasting about how great it was to be Irish. She told me curtly: "You are not Irish, you are American. Act like it!"

The black man's worst enemy is not racism

(originally published in July 1992)

The recent riots in L.A. following the acquittal of four white L.A. police officers accused of beating black motorist Rodney King are yet another symptom of a serious disease in American society. No, the disease is not racism, although I'm sure the political opportunists will try to further their power bases by exploiting the racism issue. The disease is the same one we have editorialized against in the past: Too much power in this country is now vested in our government, too little in the citizens!

The acquittal of the four L.A. police officers astounded me. It looked like an open and shut case of police brutality, judging by what I saw on the videotape. But if the jury who acquitted them erred, it is one of many mistakes a justice system is bound to make. (Sometimes, to satisfy a mob's cry for punishment, they send the wrong people to jail.) We have to live with their decision under our laws, and it does not justify the resulting riots, looting, and especially the random attacks on innocent motorists who just happened to be in the neighborhood.

Nevertheless, I sympathize with some of the rioters. Not the lawless bands of thugs and gang members who comprised the majority of the rioters, but with some of the ordinary blacks who, like you and me, can only be pushed so far before they push back, however so blindly.

Many blacks are locked into inner city poverty with little hope of ever getting out. There are a variety of reasons why this is so, including prejudice from the rest of us, but the main reason is that government has destroyed the black family with a welfare check.

"Do-gooder" social engineers have created third and fourth generation welfare recipient families by offering black mothers more money than their jobless husbands can provide. The result is that 80% of L.A. black children grow up without a father figure in the home. Without a proper father figure, black children are at an extraordinary disadvantage. Many are forced to learn the ways of the world on the streets, and if their fathers do happen to come home, the cops and the D.A. are waiting to arrest them for failure to pay their child-support payments.

The major foe of blacks in the inner cities of America is not racism or bad court decisions, but the friendly faced "do-gooder" bureaucrat with his easy welfare money. That bureaucrat doesn't say, "Here's some opportunity to help you get on your feet and into the mainstream of society." He says, "Here's some money; go enjoy yourself and leave everything to me." Then he goes back to his cushy job, secure in the knowledge that his job is safe because blacks don't have a prayer of getting out of poverty with such a dependency system. The problem with black families in L.A., and in most urban cities, is that welfare bureaucrats have taken over their lives. They've hooked many on welfare, promising them ever-increasing benefits if only they'll vote for politicians that keep the bureaucrats in their jobs. Who wouldn't fall for such a trap? The wonder is that so many blacks do overcome this pernicious dependency system and make it on their own.

And when a gutsy black does make it on his own, what happens? A good look at the confirmation hearings of Supreme Court Justice Clarence Thomas will give you an idea. The politicians who depend on black impoverishment as part of their power base went after him like coyotes after a domestic dog who has strayed too far from home. They tried to rip out his guts. They accused him of being prejudiced against his own people because he had disdained the welfare system and all the other white bureaucratic "do-gooder" traps. They couldn't stand an "uppity black" telling them to shove their welfare programs. The judge saw the "free money" programs for what they were—dead end roads designed by social engineers who don't understand that we live in a society in which the individual must learn to cope on his own.

The real tragedy of the riots in L.A. is that they will probably be used by misguided social engineers and opportunistic politicians to convince government to pour more money into the same welfare programs that have destroyed black families for generations.

People don't need welfare bureaucrats running their lives; they need jobs and their own small businesses so they can stand up by themselves. The way you create jobs is by giving small businesses a climate in which they can flourish. Rather than tax businesses to death to feed counterproductive government bureaucracies like the welfare system, encourage small businesses to open in the inner cities, or within traveling distance of the inner cities. Rather than offer bigger checks to welfare recipients and fatter retirement benefits to welfare administrators, offer incentives to black entrepreneurs. Rather than give the black mother a cash replacement for her husband, give the black man the opportunity to come home to his family.

I'm proud to be a "Losertarian"

(originally published in January 2007)

After the recent midterm elections, in which Democrats wrested control of both houses of Congress from Republicans, I was listening to the Michael Medved national radio talk show as he was blaming "Losertarians" for the Republican defeat. I am, of course, one of the Libertarians to which he was referring and, like most of my fellow Libertarians, I voted for the best candidate I could find, some of whom happened to be Libertarians. Libertarians at the national level lost, as they usually do, but some won at the local level, as they often do.

Medved, whose show this magazine has sponsored in the past because he shares a few Libertarian views, was particularly livid about the fact that Montana Libertarians delivered just enough votes to the Libertarian candidate in that state to deliver the Senate seat to the Democrat candidate, thereby delivering the control of the U.S. Senate to the Democratic Party. Medved presumed that those Libertarian voters would have voted for the Republican candidate had there been no Libertarian candidate on the ballot, and he was probably correct since there are more Republicans than Democrats who stand for limited Government.

But, that's beside the point. As a Libertarian who forsook his Libertarian leanings and voted Republican the last two

Presidential elections, I am delighted Libertarians had a hand in throwing the Republicans back out in the street. They were as worthless as the Democrats they had previously replaced. In fact, they behaved worse than Democrats, spending more money than their predecessors and passing more laws that restricted the freedoms of Americans. Plus, they mismanaged the war in Iraq, bungled social security reform, screwed up immigration reform, and forgot all about tax reform. Seldom has there been a party that promised so much but delivered so little.

I had previously voted for Bush because he convinced me that he was for limiting Government, controlling spending, and protecting Constitutional freedoms, things which are important to Libertarians. His actions and the actions of the Republican-controlled Congress showed me he was for none of that, so it's time for them to take a hike. Forget second chances; they had their chance for 12 long years, and Government today is bigger and more oppressive than it has ever been.

I don't expect any improvement in Government from Democrats. They sure haven't delivered in the past. They'll probably go on a witch hunt and try to indict as many Republicans as they can, even try to impeach Bush. Then, in two years, it will be time to throw them out of office, too. Republicans, then Democrats; Republicans, then Democrats. What's the point? I'm done with my experiment thinking that somehow the Republicans would embrace the important Libertarian concept of limited Government. I know Democrats won't.

The main point Medved tried to make on his talk show was that Libertarians, as well as any other voter who votes neither Republican nor Democrat, are throwing away their votes because their candidates never win at the national level. "How does it feel,

Losertarians," he shouted into his radio microphone; "you just delivered the Senate to the Democrats! Are you proud of yourselves?"

Well, Michael, I sure am proud of myself for going back to voting for the best candidate, rather than the lesser of two evils, which most voters do every election. I'd like to congratulate Montana Libertarians for also voting for the best candidate. If your vote got the Democrat elected, rather than the Republican, big deal. If it gave the Senate over to the Democrats, rather than Republicans, so what. There's not a dime's worth of difference between Democrats and Republicans, anyway, so what difference does it matter who won.

What matters, I think, is that a small number of Libertarians, as well as a small number of other people voting for their third-party candidates, voted for who they thought would do a good job. They acted as individuals, not as members of a flock supporting candidates and political parties who have done nothing election after election but increase the size of Government. Libertarians throwing their votes away? I don't think so. Libertarians stood up to be counted. We all like to talk about how we want to see Government get out of our lives, but most people vote time and time again for the same political parties who deliver bigger and bigger Government election after election. It's their votes that didn't count.

Getting what we deserve

(originally published in November 2004)

One of my favorite magazines, *reason*, has a recent cover that sums up my feelings about the current presidential race. It displays side-by-side photos of Kerry and Bush with the headline **"The good news is one of these guys will lose, The bad news is one will win."**

I finally decided to vote for Bush because I didn't want to comfort the enemy by changing the chief during our War on Terrorism. But I would rather have punished Bush by voting against him, primarily because of his Patriot Act with its warrantless searches and his spending of the public treasury like there is no tomorrow. I can halfway forgive the Patriot Act by assuming it's a temporary war-time measure, but I can't forgive his profligate spending because that steals away the future of my children.

Let me explain. Bush has already increased domestic spending by 25%, compared to Clinton's 10% for all eight years of his presidency. His biggest domestic spending spree came in the form of a $530 billion Medicare bill to give seniors prescription drugs. Nice sentiment, I guess, but Medicare and Social Security are already headed for bankruptcy, as almost every economist who is not on a political payroll will tell you. His spending sprees, which more often than not were intended to blunt Democrats' political attacks that he wasn't "doing enough" for voters, coupled with the costs of fighting the War on Terror, have turned a projected 10-year budget surplus of $5.6 trillion when he took office to a current projected 10-year budget deficit of at least $2 trillion. That's one hell of a switch.

Out-of-control spending by Bush has not only further crippled already critically ill programs like Social Security and Medicare, but it leaves our children with a projected debt that will amount to approximately $90,000 per household by the year 2014. People like me are looking to leave something for our children, not saddle them with debt.

Of course, we all know Bush didn't bring about this staggering fiscal calamity for our children all by himself. The Democrats, judging from their election year rhetoric, want to spend even more than Bush. In fact, it is remarkable in this presidential election that neither candidate talks about the imminent insolvency of programs like Social Security and Medicare, because the candidates know that to talk about the "third rail of American politics" is tantamount to committing political suicide. Which leads to the obvious conclusion that it is we, the voting public, who for years have been encouraging both political parties to spend without regard for tomorrow, who is ultimately to blame for this financial crisis.

Well, surprise to us all, the bill for these decades of spending is going to come due sooner than many of us thought. Try about five years from now when the 77 million post-World War II baby boomers begin to retire. So my generation (I was born in 1944, two years before the beginning of the baby boom bubble) will get to join in this big payback after all. And it's going to be painful.

Here's the way I see things playing out. The first few years Social Security and Medicare benefits will be paid to baby boomers as planned, but the government will begin raising payroll taxes to take the strain off the system. In a few short years, Democrats and Republicans will begin screaming at each other that they are to blame for the obvious shortfall in funds to pay for the retirement systems. There will be calls to cut benefits while raising payroll taxes even more. Elections will be won or lost strictly over who has a better fix for Social Security and Medicare, and the voting public *will have to pay attention* because it will be they who are paying taxes or getting benefits.

By 2020, payroll taxes will have to rise by 50% to pay for Social Security and Medicare benefits, and by 2040 they will have to rise by more than 200%. The taxpayers won't wait for the 2040 increases, but will revolt, either joining an underground economy or forcing legislators to repeal the Social Security cost-of-living escalator and cutting benefits. Even many retired folks will realize that the taxpayers are right, that this new generation should not have to bear the burden of a problem essentially created by the retirees themselves years before they retired.

Something will have to give. If there is a recession, all hell will break loose, and the Social Security and Medicare crisis will be on us all at once. There will be general financial chaos with politicians pointing the finger at anyone they can. The retirees will be caught in the middle of a financial catastrophe of their own doing.

And then the magic bullet will appear. People will remember the Carter years when inflation ran to 21%, and crafty politicians will crank up the government printing presses and fuel inflation to those levels again. With the Social Security cost-of-living escalator repealed, government will dole out smaller and smaller benefit increases and let inflation do its magic. It will take 20-plus years for the baby boom bubble to pass through the system, and many of them will be half starving with little relief for their medical problems. But they will pass through finally and become a footnote in history on how not to run a government retirement program.

And so justice will be served. One of the generations (mine) who helped create this retirement fiasco will be devastated by it. Their children won't get a dime from the system and will have to start from scratch. Meanwhile, I plan to begin collecting Social Security by age 62, two years from now, so I at least get something. The moral of this story? It's the same moral of every story. Take care of your own future, because no one else is going to.

Flushing toilets
with other people's money

(originally published in November 1993)

It's the season of the spendy politician, and it seems that every-one in government, from the federal level on down to the town level, is turning to tax increases as a way to solve funding prob-lems in recession-ridden economies. It's a solution that has always been favored over frugal spending by politicians, but it's a solution that is almost always wrong.

Tax schemes never get presented for what they are, namely a way to increase the influence of government over our lives. Instead they are portrayed as investments in the future—invest-ments in education, infrastructure, jobs, or whatever it takes to convince you to fork over your dough and give up some of your personal liberty to a bureaucrat. When the "investment" angle doesn't work, politicians usually try to convince the bulk of the voters that "they" won't be the ones to pay for or suffer from the tax.

All the devious strategies to convince you to pay more taxes can be dissected into their various strategical elements, so as a tax payer you may find it enlightening, possibly alarming, to see how it all works. To dissect a tax scheme designed to dupe you, you'll probably have to go no further than your own hometown.

We found ours in our hometown—Ashland, Oregon—a beautiful city of about 17,000 that is dependent, in part, on the tourists who flock here to see its excellent eight-month-long Oregon Shakespear Theatre. Here's how our local politicians pulled off their latest tax scheme:

It started earlier this year when the city council decided that it was necessary to improve the city's sewer system. A tax scheme always starts with a necessary need. Council members decided that the tax scheme to be presented to the citizens should be simple and painless, so they opted to add a 1% meals tax at local restaurants, putting the burden of the new tax, they assured voters, on the shoulders of tourists and people who can afford to eat out (the rich?).

So they put the tax measure on the ballot in a special city election. The tax, of course, had a not-so-well publicized provision that permitted council members, if their future wisdom so dictated, to raise it as high as 5%.

The tax was the main business of a special election, and the public debate for and against it was fairly furious, with all city councilors but one extolling its virtues. The lone dissenter, the astute Pat Acklin, observed, "I don't see why guests in our community should subsidize our toilet flushing."

Despite the debate, as in all special elections, only a fraction of the voters turned out so only a fraction of the citizenry got to pass a tax (55% to 45%) on everybody else. The restaurant owners who would be forced to collect the tax howled, of course, but there were too few of them, so they were ignored.

So all went well for the politicians, as it usually does in these special elections "designed" to do something "necessary and good" for the community. But then something unexpected

268

happened: Soon after the tax was passed, and nearly two months before it was to take effect, the city council voted to raise the 1% meals tax to its maximum of 5%.

But the usual good timing of the politician was way off this time. This decision caught their constituencies by surprise. In fact, when the sleepy citizens of Ashland read their newspapers the morning after the council raised the tax, many concluded that they had been duped. And as if in one voice, the voters roared, "That's not what we voted for!"

The city council's arrogance not only caused residents to support a meals tax recall measure that will go on yet another election ballot in November, but it put the entire meals tax scheme under the public microscope. People wanted to know what happened. Well, here, in a nutshell, is a dissection of the Ashland City Council meals tax into its various and devious strategies. See if it bears any resemblance to a tax scheme targeted for you.

First, the city council presented a benefit to the city's residents that they said residents wouldn't have to pay for. That should have been a tip-off. A "something-for-nothing" promise should make all consumers run like hell, but it is a ploy used regularly by politicians at all levels of government.

Second, the city council singled out a segment of their own community—restaurant owners—that was too small a group to resist a tax forced on them. "Divide and rule," said Machiavelli, and politicians do it on a regular basis.

Third, the city council made the tax small enough (1%) to be palatable by disguising the real size of the tax (5%) in a clause that could be executed later. Craftier politicians would have waited a year before increasing the tax.

Fourth, the council presented the tax in a special election. There are so many special elections in small communities that residents get weary of going to them, so the supporters of whatever is up for a vote—in this case a tax—have a better chance to march out their vote. It's simply a method of diluting the vote to your own advantage. Kid stuff, right?

The Ashland City Council did everything according to the politician's slick little unpublished book, except they got too antsy and arrogant and accidentally blew their cover.

In November, Ashland voters have a chance to repeal the meals tax and find another way to finance the flushing of their toilets. I'm sure the tourists who already contribute mightily to the local economy will be grateful. So will their neighbors, the restaurant owners.

Ashland voters' victimization by its own elected officials should be a lesson to us all, because what happened in Ashland is what is happening all over America today—politicians are convincing more and more voters to force taxes on other people to pay for government services only a few have decided are necessary. Experience teaches us that more taxes translates into nothing other than more government and, by gosh, haven't we learned yet that more government is not the solution, but the cause of most of our problems?

The people of Ashland have a smelly mess on their hands, but it isn't in their toilets. Three cheers for a community that can admit it made a mistake and head right back to the ballot box to correct it. More of us should wake up to the smell that awoke the residents of Ashland.

The politics of tragedy

(originally published in July 1995)

The bombing of the Murrah Federal Building in Oklahoma City was a national tragedy, and those who took part in it must be brought to justice. As of this writing, Timothy McVeigh, a nutcase reportedly influenced by another national tragedy—the incineration of people at the Branch Davidian Compound in Waco, Texas—is the prime suspect. But, if you believe the mass media, most conservative groups and talk radio hosts are also prime suspects. These people spread hate, the media tells us, and therefore are somehow responsible for Timothy McVeigh's hate.

President Bill Clinton himself, not one to miss a political opportunity, has been lashing out at conservative groups and talk radio hosts, insinuating that their anti-government rhetoric is what prompted a nut like McVeigh to act. The President has taken special aim at the voluntary militia groups that have multiplied like rabbits since he took office, calling them "false patriots" and paranoids who incite anti-government violence.

And, of course, the mass media is echoing the President. Our newspapers and TVs have been filled with stories about right-wing "extremist groups" that are creating a climate of hate and intolerance. Stories about illegal guns and seizures of illegal ammunition are everywhere, as if there is somehow a link

271

between them and the bombing. A media moron even asked conservative House Speaker Newt Gingrich if he thought he bore some responsibility for the climate that may have led to the bombing.

It is a media circus that is appalling to me. Here we have the killing of innocent people by some nut, and it is seized upon by the President and the mass media like it is some great political story that will give them the opportunity to show how right they have been all along in railing against conservatives and "right-wing" groups. To me it is not only unconscionable and a lie, but it is a transparent attempt to politicize a tragedy and it will backfire.

Instead of the President reaping political hay and the mass media reaping public approval for their past one-sided reporting, I think they will both reap the utter disgust many Americans feel when confronted by charlatans. And instead of recapturing the fading influence and power they both so desperately want to hang onto, they will fall deeper into public disrepute because Americans hate being lied to, especially when the lies are hidden behind a tragedy that we all feel deeply about.

The tragedy of the Oklahoma City bombing is a national calamity. We all feel sorrow for the victims, and the deaths of the 13 children there bring it home to all of us like only the deaths of innocents can. It is a horrific crime, and as a parent of four children, my heart goes out to those parents who lost theirs.

If the President and mass media want to use this tragedy to point an accusing finger, let them point it at themselves. Not for the Oklahoma City bombing, but for their failure in the past to acknowledge crimes just as horrible, and for their convenient neglect in the past to make sweeping and preposterous accusations. Two cases from the past come to mind.

The first is appropriate because the President and mass media have brought it up. It is Waco, the supposed Alamo cry of the right-wing groups that the President and mass media have been attacking. Eighty-six Branch Davidians, including 25 innocent children, died there in a fire seen on national TV after a lengthy siege by federal officers in search of illegal guns. In the wake of that tragedy, President Clinton said it should serve as a lesson to other religious cultists, and his attorney general, Janet Reno, said that if she had to, she'd do it again. There was no sympathy for the 25 children who died, no meaningful investigation of those government officials who authorized and took part in the raid, and no punishment meted out beyond letters of reprimand. The government did, however, put the survivors on trial, but when they were convicted of only minor gun charges, the judge gave them 40 years each, anyway. Victory, the government claimed. Vindication! Is it any wonder that right-wing groups are using Waco as a rallying cry for recruitment?

The second is the Unabomber, a letter-bomber killer that *Newsweek* magazine reported as espousing an "ultra-leftist, ecoterrorist agenda." The Unabomber has struck 16 times in the last 17 years. His latest victim, Gilbert Murray, a timber industry lobbyist with two children, was killed in Sacramento the month after the Oklahoma City bombing. This self-avowed liberal ecoterrorist has been on the loose for 17 years, killing and maiming innocent people. But have you heard any calls by the mass media for an investigation of environmental groups? Have any Democratic politicians been asked if they think they bear responsibility? Have you seen even a suggestion of a witch-hunt of the left, as we are now seeing of the right?

Of course not, and there shouldn't be. It is an absurd assumption to conclude that environmentalists and liberals are responsible for the Unabomber. But it is just as absurd an assumption for the mass media to conclude that conservatives are responsible for Timothy McVeigh.

And what about the innocent children who died? They died in Waco, too. Why didn't you declare a national day of mourning for them, Mr. President? Did their parents have the wrong political beliefs?

The way President Clinton and the mass media can so casually politicize tragedy is disgusting. A national day of mourning for Oklahoma City, but "we'd do it again" for Waco.

At Fascism's doorstep

(originally published in May 1999)

Fascism and Socialism are the political philosophies that hold that the state should control a country's means of producing wealth. Where Socialism seizes the money-producing industries outright, Fascism leaves much of the private sector intact but tightly controls it through government management. Otherwise, there's barely a nickel's worth of difference between the two political systems. Germany and Italy were the prime Fascist states during World War II, and Communist countries like China, Cuba, and the former Soviet Union are the modern Socialist states. These states always come to ruin, because state control of people's lives is an unworkable idea. It goes against human nature, and, historically, Fascism and Socialism have only been maintained by government force, until the enslaved and impoverished people rebel and bring down the government.

Despite Fascism's and Socialism's disastrous records, which includes not just the financial ruin of the countries that adopted them but a legacy of imprisonment and murder of millions of the citizens of the unfortunate countries, the appeal of these unworkable systems is still strong in many countries, including this one. If you want a bold new example, just take a look at President Clinton's proposal to save Social Security in America, and

275

witness the response—or rather, the lack of outrage—from Democrats and Republicans in the U.S. Congress.

Under the guise of trying to save Social Security, which accounts for nearly 22% of all federal spending, President Clinton has proposed that a large portion of Social Security trust fund money be invested by the government into the stock market to earn a greater return for future retirees. His proposal is a bastardization of financial studies that conclude that Social Security recipients would be far better off if the Social Security system were privatized, so that participants, instead of investing money into a system that nearly everyone agrees cannot survive as presently structured, were allowed to invest their Social Security tax dollars into the private sector. Among the many compelling reasons cited by these studies: The private sector has earned 8% in real money over the past 75 years (including the Depression years), while the government's Social Security has earned 2%—not in real money, but in government IOUs.

Clinton's proposal, however, would allow the government, not Social Security participants, to invest the money in the stock market, thus maintaining government ownership and control over the funds. Due to the large sums involved—about $650 billion—it would give government direct management control over nearly every major American business in America, opening the door to political pressures about how those companies do business. As has already been demonstrated by some state and county pension funds that already invest in the stock market, politics will replace sound financial management as the criterion for investment. For example, environmental companies would get lots of government investment, while tobacco companies and others who do not toe the party line would get nothing. The result would be the undermining of sound financial investment with the political expediency of investing public money into socially desirable businesses.

Incredibly, few congressmen are calling this proposal for what it is, namely, a barely veiled attempt by opportunistic politicians to subvert America's free enterprise system, which is the foundation upon which this country is built.

The Clinton plan would capitalize on Americans' fears that the Social Security system is on the verge of bankruptcy, that the Social Security trust fund has only government IOUs in it, and that their Social Security retirement money is no more secure than a White House intern in the oval office. These fears are all well-founded, because Social Security is going broke and action needs to be taken to save it. But Clinton's solution is not an attempt to save Social Security, but an attempt to inject major government control into the American economy.

Just as he attempted to nationalize one fifth of the nation's economy under the pretense of health care reform, Clinton now is attempting to put government control over American business under the guise of saving Social Security. Alarm sirens should be going off inside the heads of all freedom-loving Americans. It would mean the greatest increase in federal power since the introduction of the income tax; not even Roosevelt, at the height of the New Deal, proposed government control of American industry.

Truly privatizing Social Security by allowing participants to invest in 401K and IRA-type accounts in the private sector would not only save Social Security by dramatically increasing participants' future retirement benefits, but it would increase the country's economic growth by making more money available for investment. However, letting the government invest the money in the stock market would strangle the private sector with government control, just as government has strangled it in other state-controlled economies. Saving Social Security would then become a moot point, because the economy will have been ruined, taking Social Security along with it.

Opportunists like Clinton and his fellow Republicrats are not interested in meaningful reform. They are interested in seizing the panic of the moment to further their own misguided Socialist view of America's future. Don't let them! If Clinton can sneak this dirty trick past a gullible public and through a Congress that lacks the guts to stand up to this would-be dictator, then the American system will fall without a shot being fired. This sinister proposal places America at Fascism's doorstep.

Rewriting the Bill of Rights

(originally published in November 1992)

Russian Communists and German Nazis were the most efficient rewriters of history. Both were ruthless in the beginning, killing anyone who disagreed with the new histories that supported their peculiarly warped ideologies.

The Nazis, fortunately, were defeated in war, but the Russians (the Soviets) continued to rewrite history with ideological fervor, discovering in the process that it was easier to teach the historical lies to the nation's youths than it was to kill millions of unbelieving adults, although they did still manage to kill or forcibly reeducate millions of unbelievers.

Now that the Russian system has collapsed under the weight of its own lies, that discredited Socialist ideology seems to have found a new home—here in the United States—and the rewriters of history are at work again.

Here's one example: Eric Grig of Boone, North Carolina, went into a North Carolina bookstore and asked the clerk if he had a book on the Constitution of the United States. The clerk gave him a book titled *The Constitution of the United States* by Floyd G. Cullop. Mr. Grig sent the book to me.

Cullop, who has taught history for 17 years to junior and senior high school students in Tennessee, has a simple premise for his book: "The United States Constitution is often difficult to read and understand." So he sets out to explain it, not just with his personal opinions, but with his rewriting of what the Constitution actually says.

Here is the most glaring example: Part III of the book is titled, "The Bill of Rights." The Second Amendment, according to Cullop, is written as follows:

Amendment 2. Right to Bear Arms

For their protection and for purposes of having a well trained militia the people of the states may keep and bear (own) arms (weapons), but the federal government or the state governments may pass laws against owning certain weapons and the way others may be used.

Now, anyone casually familiar with the U.S. Constitution knows that that is not how the Second Amendment reads. It reads as follows:

A well-regulated militia, being necessary to the security of a free State, the right of the people to keep and bear arms, shall not be infringed.

However you may interpret those words, those are the words. There's nothing in it about government being able to "pass laws against owning certain weapons and the way others may be used," as Mr. Cullop asserts.

Like so many ideological zealots before him, Cullop's attempt to rewrite history—in this case the most important historical document this nation has—cannot stand up to the scrutiny of an informed adult like Mr. Grig of North Carolina, but it could easily get by a younger person, such as the junior and senior high-schoolers Cullop has been teaching for 17 years. And I think that's exactly the intention of Mr. Cullop—to hoodwink younger readers so they will grow up to believe what is simply an ideological lie.

Mr. Cullop is not unlike many in the mass media who routinely distort current events and history to promote their own ideology. In this particular case, Mr. Cullop obviously believes guns should be controlled somehow, and he knows that the only way guns can be controlled is if the Constitution is somehow distorted to read that the Government can change the Second Amendment simply by passing a law. Cullop, like the Russians, is in it for the long haul—he's hoping to pollute those young minds for the future.

To be fair, Mr. Cullop does give the real Constitution at the end of the book, long after the damage has been done.

About the author

Dave Duffy has been the publisher and editor of *Backwoods Home Magazine* since 1989 when he founded the publication. Prior to that he had been a journalist for daily newspapers in Massachusetts, Nevada, and Southern California, then a technical writer and editor for the Department of Defense in Southern California. He was born in 1944 in South Boston. His mother, Margaret McCarthy, immigrated to America from Ireland, as did the parents of his father, Walter J. Duffy. He currently lives in the mountains overlooking the southern Oregon coast with his wife and three sons.